W9-CAZ-526

HEROES OF PEARL HARBOR

Allan Zullo

SCHOLASTIC INC.

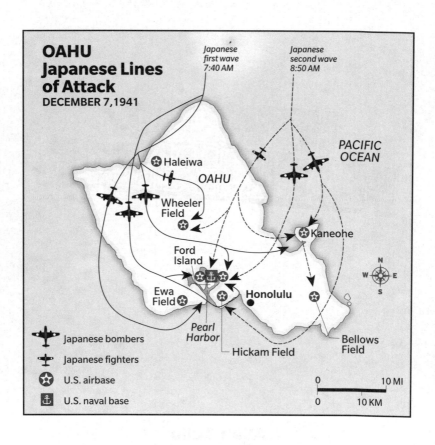

**OAHU
Japanese Lines
of Attack**
DECEMBER 7, 1941

Japanese
first wave
7:40 AM

Japanese
second wave
8:50 AM

PACIFIC
OCEAN

Haleiwa

OAHU

Wheeler
Field

Kaneohe

Ford
Island

Ewa
Field

Honolulu

Pearl
Harbor

Hickam Field

Bellows
Field

N
W E
S

Japanese bombers

Japanese fighters

U.S. airbase

U.S. naval base

0   10 MI

0   10 KM

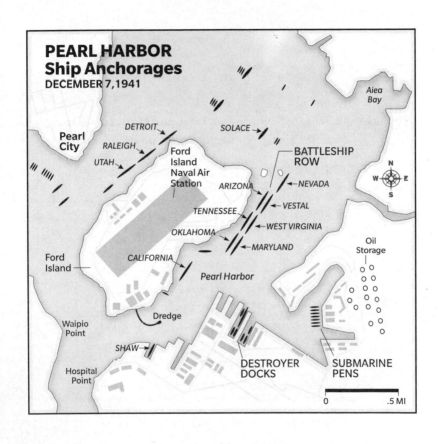

PEARL HARBOR
Ship Anchorages
DECEMBER 7, 1941

Aiea Bay

Pearl City

DETROIT

RALEIGH

UTAH

SOLACE

Ford Island Naval Air Station

BATTLESHIP ROW

ARIZONA

NEVADA

VESTAL

TENNESSEE

WEST VIRGINIA

OKLAHOMA

MARYLAND

Ford Island

CALIFORNIA

Pearl Harbor

Oil Storage

N
W E
S

Waipio Point

Dredge

Hospital Point

SHAW

DESTROYER DOCKS

SUBMARINE PENS

0   .5 MI

To Lucio and Teresita Gorospe and Trent and Mary Lou Manausa,
whose devotion to family knows no limits
—A.Z.

ISBN 978-0-545-87276-8

10 9 8 7 6 5 4 3 2 1   18 19 20 21 22

Made in Jiaxing City, China   68
First printing 2016

Book design by Cheung Tai

AUTHOR'S NOTE

You are about to read ten stories of incredible acts of heroism that took place on water, on land, and in the air at Pearl Harbor, Hawaii, on the day the Empire of Japan launched a surprise air attack against America.

As tragic as it was—2,403 Americans lost their lives—the raid brought out the best in the thousands of sailors, Marines, soldiers, and aviators who fought back under an overwhelming barrage of heavy bombs, torpedoes, and machine gun fire.

I can't write about the amazing exploits of every brave person at Pearl Harbor. However, I've singled out, as a representative sample of what happened on that infamous day, several dozen servicemen whose courageous actions are truly remarkable. They did what had to be done—no matter the risk, no matter the cost.

Each of the ten stories in this book features multiple heroes. Many of them earned the Medal of Honor—our country's highest award for valor in combat. Most of the other heroes were presented with the Navy Cross, the second-highest combat award.

These true accounts are based on memoirs, oral histories, battle reports, newspaper stories, history books, and military records and citations. Using real names and places, the stories are written as factual versions of the heroics, although some dialogue has been re-created.

For realism, the dialogue contains a word referring to the Japanese that by today's standards is considered offensive but was commonly used back then. Also, there's some mildly bad language because, well, that's the way servicemen talked in combat. You'll notice, too, that this book refers to a ship as *she* or *her*. It's an old maritime tradition that goes back centuries. Using the feminine form for a ship is still a common practice in the navy. Because there are so many naval terms used in these stories, there is a glossary in the back of the book.

So why did I write about Pearl Harbor heroes? If you've read any of the other books in my 10 True Tales series, then you know of my fondness and respect for heroes—*Heroes of Hurricane Katrina, Young Civil Rights Heroes, Vietnam War Heroes, World War I Heroes, World War II Heroes, FBI Heroes,* and *Heroes of 9/11* to name a few. Some of the most heroic moments in military history unfolded during the Pearl Harbor attack, and they are worthy of your attention if only because they make for great reading.

These heroes were everyday guys, from baby-faced "swabbies" to graying "old salts," who suddenly found themselves caught in the bull's-eye of a horrific attack. They didn't cower. They didn't hide. While bombs exploded around them, torpedoes ripped open hulls, and planes strafed them, these brave souls sprang into action. They gave their all and then some—including, in several cases, their very lives—to save their ships, to rescue their shipmates, to strike back against a merciless enemy.

They are the heroes of Pearl Harbor.

A.Z.

CONTENTS

"A DATE WHICH WILL LIVE IN INFAMY"

December 7, 1941.

Until the terrorist attacks of September 11, 2001, no date in modern American history has delivered a more painful assault to our country. For generations, the date has come to symbolize heartache and heroism, fear and courage, treachery and sacrifice.

It was the day when Japan attacked US naval ships and military bases at Pearl Harbor, Hawaii, in a devastating air assault that killed 2,403 people and provoked America into entering World War II.

Although the two countries had been at peace, tensions between them were nearing a breaking point. Alarmed by Japan's aggressive efforts to expand its empire along the western Pacific and gain control of sorely needed natural resources, the US ceased trade relations with the island nation. Japanese leaders believed the only country standing in their way of becoming a major world power was the United States, which based its large Pacific Fleet in and around Pearl Harbor on the Hawaiian island of Oahu. (At the time, Hawaii was an American territory and didn't become a state until 1959.)

Even though war had been raging in Europe for two years, the United States had remained on the sidelines because neither the White House, Congress, nor the public had an appetite for entering the armed conflict.

Japan sensed an opportunity to strike. After months of plotting and training in secrecy, Japan sent six fully loaded aircraft carriers on a mission to destroy America's military might in Hawaii. Without being detected, the carriers sailed 3,800 miles across the Pacific, escorted by two battleships, eight destroyers, three cruisers, and three submarines.

Few American military officials believed a Japanese assault on Hawaii was possible because it was so far away from Japan. As a result, early on a calm Sunday morning, the alert level was low throughout Pearl Harbor.

Most of the estimated 400 US Army, Navy, and Marine planes at the six air bases on Oahu were parked in neat rows, wingtip to wingtip. In Pearl Harbor, 70 American warships and 60 other naval vessels were anchored or moored, most with their ammunition locked up and weapons sheathed. Many of the ships had been left in the care of junior officers because the captains and senior officers had spent the night ashore, enjoying time with family and friends, and had yet to return. For most of the sailors onboard, Sunday was supposed to be a day of rest, of fun in the sun, of relaxation in paradise.

At 7:53 A.M., everything changed.

Inspired by flight commander Mitsuo Fuchida's battle cry of "*Tora! Tora! Tora!*" (Tiger! Tiger! Tiger!), Japanese pilots in 51 dive-bombers, 40 torpedo bombers, 49 high-level bombers, and 43 fighter planes known as Zeros attacked Pearl Harbor, catching Americans completely off guard.

First, the raiders roared over the airfields, blowing up hangars and blasting apart American planes that never got off the ground, to blunt US Forces from mounting an effective defense in the air.

Controlling the skies, the Japanese unleashed torpedoes, bombs, cannon fire, and machine gun fire on the heart of the US Pacific Fleet—the eight battleships that were docked along the eastern edge of Ford Island, a naval air base in the middle of the harbor.

The ships' alarms blared and loudspeakers shouted, "General quarters!" as sailors who had been sleeping, lounging, or eating breakfast scrambled to their battle stations. Some of the men arrived at their posts barefoot, half-dressed, or clad only in their skivvies in the chaotic opening minutes of the surprise attack. The sailors and Marines on the ships fought back with machine guns and antiaircraft fire but were virtually helpless against the torrent of bombs and torpedoes that slammed into the ships.

At 8:10 A.M., an armor-piercing bomb penetrated the forward deck of the USS *Arizona,* touching off more than a million pounds of gunpowder. The massive explosion sank the vessel in 9 minutes and killed 1,177 men. Minutes later, the USS *Oklahoma*, ripped open by five torpedoes, capsized. The USS *West Virginia* and the USS *California* began sinking from a salvo of bombs and torpedoes.

By 8:25 A.M., enemy planes departed Pearl Harbor, which was shrouded in heavy smoke, its waters streaking with blood and burning from flaming oil slicks. As Americans hustled to care for the wounded and remove the dead, a second wave of Japanese planes—167 bombers and fighters—attacked many of the same ships and airfields again and sought out targets that previously hadn't been damaged.

But this time, the enemy met much stiffer resistance from the damaged ships' gunners. Firing throughout the attacks, the battleship USS *Nevada* made a break for the open sea. She didn't get that far. She was hit by a torpedo and as many as ten bombs, but she stayed afloat by deliberately beaching herself. A heavily damaged repair ship, the USS *Vestal*, also avoided sinking by intentionally going aground.

Against great odds, a small group of valiant American pilots took off and attacked the raiders, shooting down at least a dozen of them. Meanwhile, in the midst of fire, explosions, and relentless strafing, courageous men made heroic efforts to save their ships and their shipmates and to blast enemy aircraft out of the sky. The brave actions led to the awarding of 15 (10 of them posthumously) Medals of Honor—the highest combat medal—and 51 of the second-highest combat medal, the Navy Cross.

About two hours after the sneak attack began, it was over. The Japanese planes returned to their carriers, leaving behind an island of death and destruction. The raid claimed the lives of 2,335 American military personnel and 68 civilians and wounded an additional 1,178 people, including 35 civilians.

Going by just the numbers, Japan scored a stunning victory while the United States suffered the worst, most humiliating naval defeat in its history. Of the estimated 400 American planes on the island, 169 were destroyed and 159 badly damaged. In Pearl Harbor, four battleships were sunk in the relatively shallow water—the *Arizona, Oklahoma, West Virginia,* and *California*—along with the USS *Utah*, a target-and-training battleship that capsized. The other battleships—the USS *Maryland*, USS *Tennessee*, and USS *Pennsylvania* (which was in dry dock)—sustained serious bomb damage. Also badly damaged were four destroyers, three cruisers, and two other ships. A harbor tug and minelayer were sunk.

Hangars, barracks, naval installations, and dry docks lay in ruins. Japan's losses are believed to be 5 midget submarines, 29 aircraft, and 64 military personnel killed and 1 captured (a submariner).

The enemy, however, failed to attack its three most prized targets—the aircraft carriers USS *Lexington*, USS *Enterprise*, and USS *Saratoga*, which were not in port at the time. Also escaping damage were the base's fuel tanks.

In Japan, news of the Pearl Harbor raid sparked wild celebration among its citizens. In the United States, the news shocked men, women, and children to their core. Not since the War of 1812 had another nation (Great Britain) attacked us on American soil. In many ways, the sneak attack in 1941 was the 9/11 for that generation.

The following day, President Franklin D. Roosevelt addressed Congress, asking for a declaration of war against Japan. He opened his address, "Yesterday, December 7, 1941—a date which will live in infamy—the United States of America was suddenly and deliberately attacked by naval and air forces of the Empire of Japan."

In his speech, Roosevelt said, "Always will we remember the character of the onslaught against us. No matter how long it may take us to overcome this premeditated invasion, the American people, in their righteous might, will win through to absolute victory." He closed by declaring, "With confidence in our armed forces—with the unbending determination of our people—we will gain the inevitable triumph, so help us God."

Three days later, Germany and Italy—having joined Japan to form the Axis powers—declared war on the United States, which had teamed up with Great Britain, Canada, Australia, the Soviet Union, and dozens of other nations in an alliance known as the Allied powers. The US was then forced to fight, along with its allies, on opposite sides of the world, in both the South Pacific and Europe.

Japan woefully underestimated the strength and resolve of the United States. After the initial waves of shock, fear, and anger swept across the land, Americans felt revived by a growing sense of unity, patriotism, and perseverance. Showing their true fighting spirit, volunteers from teenagers to those in their forties formed long lines at US Army, Navy, and Marine Corps recruiting offices. Millions were also drafted. Men and women thought of nothing else but serving their country to fight for freedom and our national honor—and to avenge Pearl Harbor.

As men went to war, women stepped into jobs they had previously never been allowed to work—in auto plants, shipyards, and factories that had been transformed into war plants. Women became supervisors, managers, and laborers. Toiling around the clock, these factories turned out hundreds of ships, thousands of tanks, hundreds of thousands of planes and military vehicles, millions of weapons, and billions of rounds of ammunition.

Whatever political and philosophical differences Americans had with one another prior to the war no longer mattered. The vast majority was united in the war effort—rationing gasoline and household supplies, salvaging metal, growing victory gardens for food, raising money through war bonds, and sending care packages to servicemen. More than 16 million Americans served during World War II to defend our country.

The US military eventually avenged Pearl Harbor. Except for the *Arizona, Utah,* and *Oklahoma,* every ship sunk or damaged that day was eventually refloated and/or repaired, and all returned to service. In the three years and nine months that America fought in the war, the navy sank every one of the

Japanese aircraft carriers, battleships, and cruisers that took part in the Pearl Harbor attack.

With US Forces leading the way, the might of the Allied powers proved too much for Japan. On September 2, 1945, Japanese officials signed surrender documents aboard the battleship USS *Missouri*, which was anchored in Tokyo Bay. Among the American warships in the bay was the very same *West Virginia* that Japan thought had been sunk for good.

It's estimated that World War II claimed the lives of 78 million military personnel and civilians, including as many as 20 million from war-related disease and famine.

Out of this deadly conflict, the United States emerged as a powerful global leader, a role it has played ever since. As unimaginable as it seemed at the time, Japan is now one of the United States's strongest allies and biggest trading partners. In remarkable displays of understanding, some Japanese aviators who took part in the raid have met with their American counterparts to forge friendships.

Although most Americans have forgiven, they will never forget. Every December 7, on National Pearl Harbor Remembrance Day, the Stars and Stripes are flown at half-staff on the White House and on government buildings to honor those who died in the attack. The day is also a reminder of Pearl Harbor's lasting impact and legacy.

Every year, nearly two million people pay homage to the fallen in visits to the awe-inspiring USS *Arizona* Memorial— a marble monument built over the remains of the sunken

Arizona—off Ford Island in Pearl Harbor. On the far side of the island, another memorial stands in front of the sunken wreckage of the *Utah,* honoring the crewmen who died trying to defend her.

Over the years, survivors often attended annual ceremonies at the memorials commemorating those who fought and died at Pearl Harbor. But because of death from old age, the number of survivors still alive in 2016—the seventy-fifth anniversary—had dwindled to an estimated 1,000 to 1,500. Eventually, there will be no servicemen who can give us their firsthand accounts, no survivors who can explain from personal experience the importance Pearl Harbor still holds today.

As Bert Stolier, a Marine who manned an antiaircraft gun at Pearl Harbor, said in 2013 when he was 93: "They call us the greatest generation. We're not the greatest generation. We had a job to do, and we did it. The greatest generation are these young people coming up today. And I hope they remember that they've got to work to keep this being the greatest country in the world."

Part of that work means understanding the significance of an important date in American history: December 7, 1941.

BAPTISM BY FIRE

Heroes of the USS *Arizona*

Radioman 1st Class Glenn Lane of the USS *Arizona* tied a towel around his neck and headed for a morning shower when he heard muffled booms. Curious, he went topside on the forecastle to investigate.

Several sailors were leaning on the lifeline, watching fireballs mushrooming up from Ford Island. At first the men thought it was a mock Army Air Corps attack that went terribly wrong. "They're using real bombs instead of dummies," a horrified seaman told Lane.

Lane looked across the harbor and saw more planes coming in low toward Battleship Row. "Oh, oh," he said. Pointing to the closest plane, he said, "That one has a fish [torpedo] on it. The army doesn't have any torpedo planes." They watched the plane drop its torpedo, which streamed toward the USS *Oklahoma*. As the plane banked sharply, Lane saw the bright red symbol of the rising sun on the underside of the wing. "Good God!" he shouted. "They're Japs!"

The plane swooped down and strafed the *Arizona*. Lane and his shipmates ducked beside a turret as bullets splintered the deck just a few feet from them. He yelled up to sailors on the bridge, "Sound the air raid! The Japs are hitting us!"

The 23-year-old radioman bolted to the deck below to warn his comrades of the Japanese assault. But the sailors didn't believe him because he was known as a jokester who spun unbelievable yarns. "Get out of here," they told him.

Not wanting to waste time arguing, he dashed toward the stern to spread the alarm—and got a similar response: "You and your jokes, Lane. You're gonna get in real trouble someday."

Just then, a dive-bomber aimed for the *Arizona* and released a bomb. It glanced off the faceplate of the No. 4 turret, toward the stern, hitting the officers' quarters. The bomb bored through three decks and then exploded, touching off several fires.

Through the smoke, Lane noticed an officer's hat laying on the deck near an uncovered hatch. Peering inside, he spotted Lieutenant Commander Samuel Fuqua, 42, who had been knocked unconscious by the blast and had fallen into a smoldering hole. Lane and another sailor climbed into it but couldn't reach Fuqua. As the stronger of the two, Lane held the ankles of the sailor who leaned into the hole and grabbed the collar of Fuqua's shirt. Then Lane pulled them both up.

Just as Fuqua was regaining consciousness, a second bomb hit farther forward, on the port side near the antiaircraft deck, throwing everyone off-balance. Moments later, another bomb blew up on the port side, triggering more fires. "Let's go! Let's go!" Lane shouted. Seeing that Fuqua was still too dazed to move, Lane shook him and said, "Crawl up the ladder, sir! Crawl up, or you'll die down here!"

Lane's strong words jarred Fuqua out of his mental fog, and he hustled up the ladder with the other seamen. The *Arizona* was a mass of flames amidships on the boat deck as yellowish smoke poured out of the open hatches from belowdecks. Sailors were sprinting in all directions. Others who were burned and in shock were crawling and stumbling out onto the deck, some with every stitch of clothing and shoes blown off or burned off them. After surveying the scene of carnage and mayhem, Fuqua told Lane and other sailors, "Quick, man the fire hoses!"

When the hoses were hooked up, the water came out in a trickle, prompting Lane to swear in frustration. The fire was spreading. Fuqua ordered, "Grab the CO_2's [fire extinguishers] on the port side. We need to hold the flames back from the quarterdeck so we can buy time to pick up the wounded."

The sailors found fourteen extinguishers and kept the fire at bay long enough for Fuqua to begin directing the evacuation of the wounded into life rafts and small boats. Looking up, Fuqua saw torpedo planes zooming in for another attack. After releasing their loads at other ships, the planes began strafing Battleship Row. But Fuqua didn't duck or seek cover. He kept helping remove the wounded, offering them words of comfort and hope, telling them, "You will survive," even when it was obvious that many wouldn't.

Then came the fourth bomb. It pierced the forward deck near the No. 2 turret about 40 feet from the bow, plowed through several decks, and landed near the magazines, which held more than a million pounds of volatile gunpowder. When the bomb detonated, it set off the powder, too, launching a fireball 500 feet in the air in a deafening explosion.

The blast was so powerful it lifted the *Arizona* several feet and shredded open the forward decks. Debris and body parts fell from the sky. The powerful force split the ship in two forward of the No. 1 turret and collapsed her forecastle decks. Like buildings in a massive earthquake, her forward turrets and the conning tower shook and then collapsed 30 feet into a huge hole. Her fuel tanks ruptured, spreading deadly fumes and oil that burst into flames throughout the ship and into the harbor.

On the bridge, Franklin Van Valkenburgh, the ship's captain, and Rear Admiral Isaac Kidd, commander of Battleship Division One, were incinerated.

The shock wave from the explosion tossed sailors out of their battle stations and flung others off the ship. Lane, who was still manning a fire hose when the bomb landed, felt a flash of unbearable heat and the stabs of shrapnel piercing his body as he was swept aft off the ship.

On antiaircraft gun No. 1, Seamen 1st Class Fred Moore, 19, and William Parker, 25, kept firing their weapon, paying little attention to the bombs falling around them. Even after the first three bombs had struck the *Arizona* and flying shrapnel and strafing fire had wounded several crewmembers, the two remained at their posts.

Although their station was now sorely undermanned, Moore and Parker continued shooting at the high-level bombers. Suddenly, two Zeros flying in tandem headed low toward the *Arizona*. The captain of the gun crew shouted, "Take cover!" But the two sailors didn't move. They were determined to destroy enemy aircraft.

But then the catastrophic fourth bomb struck. The force from the blast pitched both sailors over the side. Parker would survive. Moore wouldn't.

Despite the crippling explosion, several antiaircraft weapons and machine guns were still shooting at the enemy with undermanned, wounded gun crews.

"Lay the injured on the deck until we can get them off!" Fuqua yelled to 20-year-old Quartermaster 3rd Class Lou Conter. "And look for wounded who can't walk on their own."

Conter did what he was ordered, bringing out several injured shipmates. When he opened a hatch on the starboard side near the No. 4 gun turret, he stared into a flooded compartment and discovered four wounded sailors whose heads were barely above the water. One by one, he pulled them out. "Thanks," said one of them. "If you had come a minute later, we'd have all drowned."

Gunner's Mate 3rd Class Leland Burk was among many sailors ordered out of the turrets to fight the main fire. When he reached the quarterdeck, he was stunned by the number of wounded seamen who were sprawled everywhere, moaning and groaning for help.

Burk helped move several burn victims. To his horror, their scorched flesh came off in his hands as he carried them to rescue boats for transport to the hospital ship USS *Solace* or to Ford Island. Some of the wounded in the boats never made it—they were killed in Japanese strafing runs.

Burk soon joined a bucket brigade that was passing pails of water from one sailor to the next. Their efforts, though, did little to squelch the flames of the sinking ship. Fuqua, who was now the most senior officer onboard still alive, urged the men to "keep up the good work." But everyone knew it was futile. "Commander," said Burk, "there's no use in fighting it anymore."

Noting that all guns of the antiaircraft and secondary battery were now out of action, Fuqua nodded grimly and admitted, "She can't possibly be saved." He gave the orders to abandon ship.

Within nine minutes of the fourth bomb, the *Arizona* had settled onto the shallow bottom. Her mangled superstructure and upper decks were all that remained above the surface—and they were still burning.

*　　*　　*

After the first bomb dropped, Major Alan Shapley, the leader of the 88 Marines aboard the *Arizona,* raced toward his gunnery station on the mainmast, which was 90 feet in the air. On his way there, he shouted to several of his young Marines, "This is the real thing!" As if to emphasize the point, the deck of the fantail was being shattered by machine guns from passing dive-bombers.

While he and 13 other Marines began climbing the mainmast tripod, a bomb struck the quarterdeck, sending shrapnel and fragments whistling past the men. The force of the blast nearly blew Shapely off the ladder, but he held on. The man above him, Second Lieutenant Carleton Simensen, slumped over one of the rungs and grunted, "I've been hit."

He fell backward into Shapley, who used his free arm to hold Simensen and then, mustering all the strength he could, shoved the wounded Marine a few feet up to the searchlight platform, which was 40 feet above the deck. After realizing that shrapnel had slashed open the lieutenant's chest, Shapley looked down and saw that four of his Marines had fallen off the ladder to their deaths.

"Just go," Simensen whispered, his life slipping away. "Shoot . . . down . . . those . . . Japs."

Shapley nodded. Shouting to the remaining Marines on the ladder below him, the major ordered, "Keep climbing! We have to reach our battle station!"

A minute later, the last of the Marines on the ladder, Corporal Earl Nightingale, 20, reached the searchlight platform and found Simensen lying on his back with blood spurting out of his chest. Nightingale bent over him and, taking him by the shoulders, asked, "Is there anything I can do for you?"

Simensen stared blankly at the corporal, shook his head, and closed his eyes. The blood stopped spurting. Nightingale gently lay Simensen down and continued his climb. When he joined Shapley and the other seven Marines, the corporal said, "Simensen is dead."

They discovered that the explosions had rendered the guns inoperable. All the Marines could do from their perch was watch the destruction of the Pacific Fleet. They saw the sinking of the USS *West Virginia* and the capsizing of the USS *Oklahoma*. "We might as well get down because we're doing no good here," Shapley said.

Seconds later, the disastrous explosion from the fourth bomb violently shook the ship, torching her with sky-high flames forward of the mainmast. The heat from the blast singed the Marines' hair and seared their arms. Not seeing anything but fire below and smoke around them, Shapley thought, *We're all going to get cooked to death!*

For several terrible minutes, they were trapped with nowhere to go. But then a gust blew the smoke away from their battle station. "I'll get you out of this," Shapley said. "Let's go." The Marines started down the ladder on the port side of the mast, blistering their hands on the railings because the metal was so hot to the touch.

Reaching the torn-up, burning boat deck, Nightingale gasped when he helplessly watched badly charred sailors stagger out of the flames only to collapse and die in front of him. A dying Marine sergeant called out to his fellow Marines, "Swim for it, champions!"

Nightingale followed Shapley, who found Fuqua on the starboard side ordering sailors over the side while assisting the wounded into rafts and motor launches. *He seems so calm and composed*, Nightingale thought.

Heeding the orders to abandon ship, Nightingale took off his shoes, thinking he would jump overboard and swim to Ford Island. Before he had a chance to get himself ready, another bomb that barely missed the *Arizona* exploded, spewing a huge geyser. The concussive force tossed Nightingale, Shapley, and the other Marines in their small group overboard.

"There's burning water up ahead," Shapley told them after they resurfaced. "When you get to the flames swim underwater, and when you come up for air twirl around so you won't catch fire. Then go back underwater as fast as you can." Pointing to an exposed pipeline that was halfway between the ship and Ford Island, he said, "Head for that pipe."

Trying to swim through oil—especially the sections that were on fire—was a challenge for the men. Some had shrapnel wounds and were physically and mentally exhausted. Others were just poor swimmers. So the 38-year-old athletic Shapley swam alongside them, shouting encouragement: "Be strong! Just be strong! We can do this! We're Marines!"

Inspired by his words, they swam past floating bodies and bobbing debris and slipped under the surface whenever Japanese planes strafed them. Bombs exploding nearby caused strong vibrations in the water that made the Marines' flesh jiggle.

Swimming under a burning oil slick, Shapley ran out of air and had to surface amid the flames for a few gulps. He stayed up a few seconds too long because the back of his shirt and pants caught fire.

When Nightingale was halfway to the pipe, the weight of his clothes had sapped his strength. *I can't go on*, he told himself. He started to sink.

Seeing the young corporal in distress, Shapley swam to Nightingale and told him, "Come on, son, you can do it."

But Nightingale couldn't. He was totally drained. As the corporal slid under the surface, Shapley grasped him by the shirt, pulled him up, and said, "Hang on to my shoulders." Nightingale threw his arms around the major, who then swam toward the pipeline. Even though Shapley was in superb physical shape, the extra weight from lugging Nightingale slowed him down, and he began to flounder.

Realizing that the major's strength was giving out, Nightingale loosened his grip on him and said, "Go, and make it alone. Save yourself. I'm too much of a burden."

Shapley spun around and clutched the front of Nightingale's shirt. Breathing heavily while treading water, the major said, "I'm not . . . letting go . . . of you . . . We'll make it . . . together." Willing himself to continue, Shapley began doing the side stroke while towing Nightingale. As his straining muscles throbbed in pain, the exhausted major hauled the young Marine slowly but steadily to the pipeline.

As they flopped onto the large pipe, trying to catch their breath, Nightingale squeezed Shapley's arm and murmured, "I would've drowned if it hadn't been for you."

The repair ship USS *Vestal*, which was moored beside the *Arizona*, was in serious danger of burning to the waterline unless she could break away. Parts of her deck and superstructure were already on fire from the *Arizona*'s flaming debris.

Seeing that the *Vestal* was still tethered to his battleship, Aviation Machinist Mate 1st Class Donald Graham told himself, *I can't save my ship, but I can help save the* Vestal.

Ignoring the flames that were licking at his back, and refusing to take cover under vicious machine gun fire from enemy planes strafing the deck, Graham single-handedly released all the lines that he could. Minutes later, the damaged, smoldering *Vestal* was able to get under way.

Boatswain's Mate 2nd Class Harold Smith, 25, climbed into an unmanned motor launch that was drifting aimlessly because its operator had been killed during a strafing attack. While dodging bullets and bombs, he scooped up sailors who were laboring to stay afloat. Skirting around blazing oil slicks, Smith also transported the wounded from the *Arizona* to an air-station landing. Several times he jumped in the water to rescue drowning shipmates. Those were the major victories. But there were heartaches, too—like the times when he couldn't reach a sailor who had been hollering for help before disappearing below the surface for good.

When told to abandon ship, Ensigns Henry Davison and William Bush, Yeoman 2nd Class Martin Bruns, and Aviation Ordnance Mate 2nd Class Ed Wentzlaff hopped into small boats and carried away the wounded and rescued shipmates in the burning waters.

Wentzlaff, who was one day away from the end of his three-year enlistment period, had plans to go into the resort business in Wisconsin after his discharge. But he knew he wasn't leaving the navy any time soon, now that the United States had been dragged into World War II.

Somersaulting off his ship from the horrendous explosion of the fourth bomb, Glenn Lane had trouble determining up from down for several scary seconds while underwater. When he thrashed his way to the surface, he found himself in a three-inch-thick oil slick. Gagging and coughing, he looked at the enormous flames shooting up from the main deck of the *Arizona* and thought, *This must be what the gates of hell look like.*

The towel he had tied around his neck just before the attack began was still snug under his chin. While treading water, he spun around, trying to figure out where to go. Sailors swimming near him were wondering the same thing. "What about Ford Island?" one of them said.

"I don't think I can make it that far," Lane replied.

"Our ship?"

"No sense going back there," Lane said. "It's done for."

He pointed to the USS *Nevada*, which was moored aft of the *Arizona* and was preparing to get under way even though she was damaged by two bombs and a torpedo. Lane said, "I think our best move is to swim to the *Nevada* and board her."

He and three sailors swam to the gangway, which was decorated with snow-white canvas and frills of white linen and was leaning over the side. As the sailors climbed aboard, they left an oozing trail of oil that was dripping off their bodies, prompting Lane to joke to the others, "If the boatswain mates see this, they might shoot us."

Once aboard the *Nevada*, Lane helped one of her crewmen maneuver a five-inch secondary gun. By this time, the ship was steaming away from Battleship Row. But in making her run, she drew the attention of the enemy. More bombs battered the ship, putting many of her guns out of commission, including the one that Lane was manning. Seeking shelter in casemate No. 1, he pounded on the door, but the sailors on the other side wouldn't allow him to enter. Bigotry existed in the navy, and they mistook him for a black mess attendant because of his oil-covered body and singed black hair.

Lane scurried to an adjoining casemate and received a similar reaction from these seamen, who assumed he was African American. Thinking quickly, he removed the towel from around his neck. When they saw his bare white skin that had been covered by the towel, they let him in.

No sooner had Lane stepped foot in the compartment than another bomb hit the ship directly through casemate No. 1, killing everyone inside. Feeling goose bumps crawling on his arms, he thought, *If they had let me in there, I'd be dead.*

Lane began carrying the wounded to the main deck and helping them into life rafts. Then he assisted in fighting fires. Because there was no water for the hoses, he and other sailors dragged mattresses from flooded compartments, dropped them over the flames, and stomped on them. He continued hauling up soggy mattresses until he became so fatigued that he passed out.

After regaining consciousness, he started to wash the oil off his arms, but stopped when he saw the skin was coming off, too. *Good God, my arms are charred!* Because his adrenaline had been pumping, he wasn't aware at first that he had been severely burned. The realization acted like a switch that turned on the pain. In instant agony, Lane slumped to the floor in the corner of a workshop belowdecks where he suffered alone, choking and nearly blinded by the smoke and fumes. He was later found by a corpsman, who gave him a shot of morphine to blunt the pain.

Lane was taken to the hospital ship *Solace,* where he was treated for burns and shrapnel wounds. The first doctor to examine him said, "You're a lucky young man. If you hadn't been blown into the water after the fireball, you would've been roasted."

Seaman 1st Class James Lancaster had been blown into the water by the fourth bomb that struck the *Arizona.* Gasping for breath when he resurfaced, he looked around. The water was on fire. The *Arizona* was on fire. Other ships were on fire. Ford Island was on fire. Gazing up, he saw enemy planes howling in their unrelenting attack.

What scared him the most were the terrible screams of men in agony, burned beyond recognition, some pleading for help and others begging for death to put them out of their misery.

Flames from the oil-laced water crept closer to Lancaster. Diving under the burning water, he reached a small boat and was pulled inside by a few sailors who, like him, were suffering burns and shrapnel wounds. When he felt his head, he discovered that his hair had been burned off. Although he was in pain, he started reaching for other survivors in the water. Leaning over the side, he yanked aboard barely conscious, seriously injured sailors, all the while believing, *If I can get them ashore, then they'll live.*

After transporting ten men to Ford Island, Lancaster made a second trip and helped rescue seven more faltering sailors from the water. But for each rescue, he passed triple the number of floating bodies—including a couple of his buddies who the previous night weren't convinced when he told them the ships in Pearl Harbor were "sitting ducks" for a Japanese attack. Now he would never see his pals again.

The amount of death Lancaster saw unleashed a loud anguished cry that left his throat sore. He began babbling incoherently. When his boat dropped off the second group of survivors, Lancaster tried to go out again. But an officer stopped him, saying, "You're out of your mind, and you're not thinking straight."

Onboard the *Arizona*, Fuqua continued to assist the wounded. Often he stopped what he was doing to rush over to a blinded sailor who was stumbling about and guided him over to a boat. Others were in such shock they remained frozen and unable to function, so Fuqua calmly talked to them and pulled them out of their mental paralysis. "Over the side, boys, over the side," he told them.

Under Fuqua's direction, Seaman 2nd Class Oree Weller was laying the severely injured on the quarterdeck, with rolled-up T-shirts under their heads. One of his buddies, Seaman 2nd Class Charles Brittan, 17, who had gone to boot camp with him, was brought up from a smoldering compartment and laid on the main deck. Weller bent down and cringed when he saw much of Brittan's body had turned into a crisp. His eyes were burned and his skin was blackened. Weller recognized him only because of a small tattoo, no larger than a 50-cent piece, on his right shoulder. It was of a bird in flight. "I'm here for you, Charlie," Weller told him. Those were the last words Brittan ever heard.

When the *Arizona*'s guns went silent, Boatswain's Mate 2nd Class John Anderson told a fellow sailor, "If those guys are dead, who's defending us from those planes up there?" Anderson's twin brother, Jake, was an antiaircraft gun captain. Wanting to find his brother, John climbed a ladder toward an upper deck, but the damage was too severe to reach Jake's battle station. John returned to a deck that was a foot below the surface just as a small boat, known as the captain's gig, pulled up. It was riddled with bullets and smeared in fuel oil, but it still was operating.

"Start moving the wounded into the boat," Fuqua ordered Anderson and several other sailors. "There's no time to spare."

Anderson, who was smarting from several burns and was clad only in his skivvies, helped fill the boat. While carrying a wounded sailor onto the gig, Anderson felt a hand on his back. Fuqua was nudging him from behind. "Go with the rest of them," the officer ordered. "It's time to abandon ship."

"Sir, I'm not going," Anderson replied. "My brother is still here and I've got to find him."

"Do you hear me, sailor?" Fuqua said, his voice rising. "Abandon ship before any more of us are killed!"

Fuqua shoved Anderson back into the boat and ordered

the coxswain to cast off. As the boat moved away, a sailor who was still assisting Fuqua on the *Arizona* asked him, "When are you going to get off this ship?"

Replied Fuqua, "Not until the Japs leave."

As the gig headed to Ford Island, John was sick with worry about Jake and determined to find him. Shortly after arriving on the island, he spotted a small boat drifting offshore. Turning to a friend of his, Boatswain's Mate 1st Class Chester Rose, Anderson pointed to the bobbing craft and said, "My brother is still on the *Arizona*. I'm going back. Want to come with me and look for him and anyone else left behind?"

"I'm game," Rose replied.

They waded out to the boat, motored to the burning ship, and climbed aboard. Her main deck was awash and parts of the superstructure were still in flames. The ship appeared deserted. Jake's battle station had been located on the main-mast, which was now crumpled and burning. *No one could be alive there*, John thought. He called out Jake's name as he franti-cally searched for his brother. And then he heard a weak, raspy voice respond, "Here! We're over here!"

Anderson's hopes soared that he had found his brother. "I'm coming!" he shouted back. "Keep talking." He followed the voice, which led him to the aft deck, where three badly injured sailors were propped up against the bulwark. Anderson's heart sank. None of them was Jake.

But he took some small comfort in finding three shipmates

who were still alive. One by one, he and Rose loaded the men onto the boat.

On their way to Ford Island, however, another wave of Japanese planes let loose their reign of terror. One of them descended until it was skimming the surface and then opened fire on the boat. Bullets shattered the craft wide open, and all five men spilled into the water. Almost in shock, Anderson floated in the water and checked his body. Miraculously, he wasn't hit. *Where are the others?* he thought. *I've got to find them.* "Rose! Rose, where are you?" He spun around, looking in vain for any of his shipmates, his eyes glued to the surface, hoping to see air bubbles or ripples. But there was nothing. *They're gone. They're all gone.*

Stunned by the cruel turn of events—*Would four sailors still be alive if I hadn't gone back to search for Jake?*—he swam to the island. He felt crushed. But then his heartache turned to anger. *I've got to find a way to fight back.*

He trudged inland, not knowing where he was headed or what he would do. In a stroke of luck, he found a Springfield rifle and two bandoliers of ammunition (about 200 rounds) hanging from a tree where somebody had left them. Anderson loaded the weapon and kept walking until he reached a small bomb crater. He hopped in and, with his finger on the trigger, told himself, *We'll get even with those Japs. Oh, yes, we will.*

The attack of the Arizona *remains the greatest tragedy in the history of the United States Navy, claiming the lives of 1,177 souls,* including 73 Marines. Only 335 men, including 15 Marines, survived. Among the dead were 23 sets of brothers, a father and his son who both were serving onboard, and also the Arizona's entire 21-man band. The ship's death toll accounted for nearly half of all military personnel killed during the raid.

The wreckage of the Arizona remains in place where she sank and is a national historic landmark. To honor those who perished, The USS Arizona Memorial was built in 1962 over the sunken hull of the battleship without touching it. Accessible only by boat, it's visited by nearly two million people a year. Incredibly, after more than seven decades, the Arizona still leaks nine quarts of oil every day into the harbor in what many refer to as her "black tears."

For his actions on the day of attack, Samuel Fuqua was awarded the Medal of Honor. After serving 30 years in the navy, he retired as a rear admiral. Franklin Van Valkenburgh, the ship's captain, and Rear Admiral Isaac Kidd were awarded the same medal posthumously.

Alan Shapley earned the Silver Star—the third-highest military combat medal—for his gallantry that day. He later was awarded the Navy Cross for extraordinary heroism while leading an assault against enemy forces on the island of Guam.

Awarded the Navy Cross for their actions were Donald Graham, Jim Miller, William Parker, Harold Smith, and Fred Moore (posthumously).

Glenn Lane, whose career in the navy spanned 30 years and 3 wars, often spoke about Pearl Harbor to students. When people praised him for being a hero, he'd say, "No, the real heroes are still down in the ship." After Lane died in 2011 at the age of 93, his remains were interred in the Arizona's No. 4 gun turret. He joined more than three dozen Pearl Harbor survivors who, upon their deaths, have been reunited eternally with the shipmates who perished in the attack. Edward Wentzlaff is among those whose ashes are interred there.

On December 7, 2014, four of the nine remaining Arizona survivors of the Pearl Harbor attack—John Anderson, Lauren Bruner, Louis Conter, and Donald Stratton—arrived at the USS Arizona Memorial for their last official reunion there. They gave a final champagne toast to their fallen shipmates. One of the glasses was given to a navy diver, who placed it next to the No. 4 gun turret. Said Conter, "It was an honor to toast the 1,177 shipmates who died that day. And the glass, which is now interred here, will give us a chance to have something to drink out of when we're buried here."

WHEN FORTUNE FAVORED THE BRAVE

Heroes of the USS *Vestal*

It all happened in a millisecond.

Commander Cassin Young was belting out orders from the bridge of his ship when a supersonic blast wave from a powerful explosion swept him off his feet and flung him high above the deck. His mind couldn't catch up to the speed of reality. The flash of light, the deafening roar, the giant invisible hand that swatted him like a gnat. None of that computed in his brain. Neither did the sight of chunks of steel and debris hurtling around him, nor the sailors flying in the air with him, their limbs flailing about as if they were rag dolls that had been shot out of a cannon.

Young also couldn't process the havoc wreaked on his innards from the tremendous energy released by the explosion: lungs squeezing, ears popping, stomach twisting, ligaments and joints stretching and contracting. He felt nothing, nothing at all, because he was dazed and in shock.

He was soaring off the starboard side of the USS *Vestal*, the ship he captained, and away from the USS *Arizona*, the battleship that had just blown up with such ferocity. But then gravity took hold. As the trajectory of Young's body curved downward toward the water, his brain was finally able to turn out a thought—a chilling one: *Am I about to die?*

Cassin "Ted" Young was born to be a naval officer. He was named after his ancestors, John Cassin, a navy commander during the War of 1812, and John's son, Stephen Cassin, a navy captain who was honored by Congress for his bravery during that same conflict.

After graduating from the United States Naval Academy in 1916, Young served on several battleships and submarines before being promoted to commander and becoming an executive officer of a submarine division based in Connecticut in 1939.

Well liked by his men, Young was a stickler for doing the right thing—even though such a conviction hurt his naval career. The wife of the new commanding officer wanted their house remodeled, but Young, who was responsible for the base's budget, turned down the request because the quarters had recently been renovated. "If you want it done," Young told the new captain, "you will have to sign off on the order because I, in good conscience, can't." The miffed captain retaliated by giving Young a bad evaluation report, which denied him a promotion to captain. Instead of being assigned to a fighting ship like a destroyer, Young was given command of the repair ship *Vestal*.

The 465-foot vessel carried a crew of about 600 of the navy's jacks-of-all-trades who were responsible for maintaining and repairing ships. The *Vestal* sported a foundry and complete shops for machinists, electricians, pipe fitters, blacksmiths, welders, carpenters, and other tradesmen. In her holds were sheets of steel and metals of all sizes and shapes, along with nuts, bolts, screws, rivets, and thousands of spare parts.

When the 46-year-old Young took command of the *Vestal* in 1940, he made a point of introducing himself to each member of the crew. "Hello, sailor, how are you doing?" he'd say before asking a few follow-up questions. The men admired their short, stocky leader, and also respected him because he demanded the best out of them. If he was disappointed about being given command of a humble repair ship, he didn't show it. Young concentrated on turning the *Vestal* into the best repair ship in the entire navy and instilling in his crewmen the belief that they could fix practically anything on any vessel.

On Saturday morning, December 6, the *Vestal* maneuvered into position and tied up to the outboard side of the *Arizona* in Battleship Row, the ships facing opposite each other on their port sides. About 100 job orders were piled on the desk of the *Vestal*'s repair officer, representing a week's worth of maintenance on the Pacific Fleet's largest battleship.

Young came aboard the *Arizona* to pay his respects to her skipper, Franklin Van Valkenburg, and Rear Admiral Isaac

Campbell Kidd. Young's right-hand man, Ensign B. C. Hesser, visited the battleship's chief engineer to discuss the work orders.

Meanwhile, aboard the *Vestal*, crewmen were still talking about the previous night's boxing matches at the navy yard's Bloch Center. Their man, Boatswain's Mate Joe George, had shown off his skills in the ring with another knockout. That was no surprise, considering George was a Golden Gloves boxer and three-time navy heavyweight champ.

Seamen 1st Class and best friends Paul Urdzik and John Parker were wondering how to celebrate their second anniversary in the navy. Both had enlisted on the same date— December 7, 1939. "Hey, Urdz, we should do something special on Sunday," Parker said.

"We're getting liberty [shore leave] Sunday, so let's make the rounds and hoist a few beers," Urdzik suggested.

On Sunday shortly before 8 A.M., Joseph Carroll, a 24-year-old machinist, was waiting on the *Vestal*'s main deck to board a small boat that would take him and fellow Catholic and sailor Ray Kerrigan to Mass on shore. Knowing Kerrigan's party-boy reputation, Joe George ribbed, "Hey, Carroll, you're getting a medal. You got this Irishman to go to church three Sundays in a row."

Carroll and Kerrigan assumed the planes zooming over Ford Island were American. The pair still hadn't comprehended that the bullets were real, not wooden; that the planes were Japanese, not American; that this was a sneak attack, not a realistic training mission. Then, as a plane passed over them, Kerrigan moaned, clutched his stomach, and collapsed.

"Appendicitis?" Carroll asked innocently.

Pharmacist's Mate 2nd Class Lionel Baker rushed over and kneeled next to the sprawled sailor. "He's been shot," Baker said to the others. "A bullet went into his stomach and out his back." Judging by the size of the wound, Baker knew it was fatal.

"My God, we're under attack!" Carroll exclaimed. He sprinted toward one of the guns to help man it.

Planes began diving at the *Vestal*, strafing the ship and mowing down several sailors who had failed to find cover in time. Baker hurried from one fallen seaman to another, desperately trying to use whatever he could, including the shirt off his back, to stem the bleeding.

While he was tending to an injured sailor, another plane came in low over the *Vestal* on a strafing run. Baker didn't flee and continued to aid his shipmate. But then Baker took a bullet in his shoulder and slumped over. Gritting his teeth, he went back to treating crewmen who had just been shot.

When Young heard the planes, he bounded out of his room and sprinted for the bridge. He looked up at the swarm of dive-bombers and fighter planes and began barking orders. At 8:05 A.M., the *Vestal*'s weapons—a few five-inch guns, a three-inch gun, and two .30-caliber machine guns—began firing. Young personally took command of the three-inch gun and drew a bead on a plane that flew so close he could see the pilot's teeth. Bullets from the plane ripped into the deck and pinged off the steel plates as it roared over the ship unscathed. Young was furious because his gun had jammed.

Young and his gun crew cleared the breech and fired another round, when a bomb crashed into the *Vestal* on the starboard side and exploded, igniting several fires in the lower forward hold and severing electric cables. Then another bomb struck the ship on the port side toward the stern, causing major damage to the workshops and berthing quarters belowdecks and rupturing a fuel tank. The bomb also opened up a five-foot-by-five-foot ragged hole near the bottom of the hull, causing several compartments to flood with fuel and water.

Young hurried to the bridge. He figured the high-level bombs that struck the *Vestal* were meant for the *Arizona* because she, unlike his ship, was a prize target for the Japanese. But it made no difference. His ship was in trouble, especially because the forward magazine, where nearly 700 rounds of ammunition were stored, was close to the blaze. To prevent the heat from setting off the ammo, he ordered the magazine compartment flooded.

The captain learned the engine room was taking on water from the second bomb. The damage-control crew was working feverishly to brace and shore up the leaking, bulging bulkheads to prevent them from collapsing and flooding the engines.

Young realized that being moored to the *Arizona* could

spell doom for the *Vestal*, so he wanted to cut the lines and move his ship away. But first he needed to contact his chief engineer for a damage assessment of the engine room to see if the ship was even capable of operating under her own power. Because the bomb had cut communications, Young sent a messenger.

While Young waited for a reply, he remained exposed on the bridge, directing dozens of sailors topside who were shooting at enemy planes, putting out fires, and tending to the wounded. That's when the fourth bomb struck the *Arizona*, touching off the massive explosion never before seen in naval history.

The *Vestal*, which was only 70 feet away, was shaken violently. The blast wind swept across the deck and bridge of the *Vestal* and picked up dozens of seamen—including Young—who were out in the open and pitched them in the air, over the deck and into the water.

Chunks of hot metal, burning globs of oil, and parts of bodies from blown-up *Arizona* sailors rained down on the deck of the *Vestal* and on those who had been flung into the water. The flaming debris and oil ignited new blazes both fore and aft on the ship.

Carroll was one of the lucky ones topside who wasn't swept off the *Vestal*. But he was pelted by items from the *Arizona*'s crew store, including toothpaste tubes, shaving cream cans, razor blades, and soap.

Black, choking smoke drifted over from the raging fires on the *Arizona*, making it difficult for anyone on the *Vestal* to see. Oil from the battleship's ruptured fuel tanks had caught fire and was spreading on the water toward the repair ship.

To the crewmen still aboard the *Vestal*, their ship, like the sinking *Arizona*, seemed destined for a watery grave. Their captain and dozens of fellow sailors had been blown overboard. No one knew how many—if any—seamen had survived the deck-clearing blast wave. The only certainties were that their damaged vessel was on fire, she was taking on water, and she was starting to list.

With their commander somewhere in the burning water—maybe dead, maybe not—the executive officer, who was the highest-ranking man onboard at that moment, wanted to prevent further loss of life, so he gave the orders to abandon ship. Sailors began jumping off the vessel.

Urdzik and Parker were helping reinforce the buckling bulkheads belowdecks near the engine room, when a sailor burst into the compartment and breathlessly reported, "We're abandoning ship!" A warrant officer ordered Urdzik, Parker, and the others in the room, "Let's get out of here!"

Remarkably, almost all the crewmen who had been blown off the *Vestal* by the blast wave had survived and were now bobbing in the water, trying to recover. During their flight overboard, some had been momentarily knocked out; others had been in a stupor. Once they collected their wits, many sailors swam toward Ford Island or hailed passing boats that were searching for survivors.

When Young surfaced, he wiped the oil from his eyes. Treading water, he cleared his head and looked around. Once he got his bearings, he didn't spend so much as a second pondering whether he should wait to be rescued or swim to shore. No, he had only one thought, one desire, and one plan of action: *I must return to my ship.*

His head pounding, muscles aching, and nostrils burning, Young swam through the goo, avoiding the flames, until he reached the *Vestal*'s accommodation ladder. As he emerged from the oily water, he looked like a sea creature covered in black gunk. Climbing the ladder, he was met by several sailors, led by Carroll, who were going down it.

"Sir, you're alive!" Carroll said in surprise.

Young growled, "Where do you men think you're going?"

"We've been ordered to abandon ship, sir," Carroll replied.

"Like hell," the captain snapped. "Return to your battle stations, all of you!"

After arriving on the deck, he bellowed to the sailors who had jumped into the water, "Get back onboard! No one is going to abandon ship on me!"

Those in the water who were within earshot of the captain immediately swam back through the oil slicks to the *Vestal*. Dozens, though, including those who had jumped overboard, had already reached the island or had been picked up by passing boats.

Striding across the bloody, smoking, rubble-strewn deck, Young paid no attention to the bombs that were still exploding around him, nor to the constant strafing that was plaguing Battleship Row. He gathered his officers and told them in no uncertain terms, "I'm not giving up on my ship."

As Urdzik and the others below were scrambling up to the main deck to flee the ship, they heard the topside public address system announce, "All hands, return to your battle stations!"

"Back to the engine room, lads!" hollered a warrant officer.

Breaking the tension, Parker slapped Urdzik on the back and joked, "Boy, Urdz, they sure gave us some kind of anniversary celebration, didn't they?"

Before heading to the bridge, Young helped direct crewmen in fighting fires and rescuing sailors—many of them burned—from the *Arizona* who had been blown off their ship by the blast.

On his way to the bridge, he hollered encouragement to his gunners. "Knock them out of the sky, lads!" he shouted. One of the machine gunners on the wing of the bridge fired at a low-flying Zero that was coming directly at the *Vestal*. The plane burst into flames, sputtered, and crashed on the other side of Ford Island. "Now you're cooking with gas!" yelled the captain, uttering a common term of the times for "well done."

His ship, however, was surrounded by flaming oil pouring from the *Arizona*'s ruptured tanks. And because the *Vestal* was tied to the battleship, she was still in jeopardy of getting struck by a stray bomb like the two that had already severely damaged her.

I must save her, Young thought. *We have to get away from the* Arizona.

Fortunately, the chief engineer and his "black gang"—the nickname given to crewmen who worked in the engine room (first used in the days of coal-fired steamships)—were back at work. The engineer reported they had saved the engine room from flooding. Although the steering gear was destroyed, the ship could operate under her own power. However, it would be quite limited because she was losing steam from broken pipes caused by the bombs. Normal steam pressure for getting under way was 250 pounds, but the best the black gang could get was 50 pounds—barely enough for the main engine to propel the ship.

"We'll steer by using the engines only," Young told Ensign Hesser. "We have to move her out of harm's way. There's no time to spare. Have the crew cut the lines. We're getting this ship under way."

On the *Arizona*, Seaman 1st Class Donald Stratton, Boatswain's Mate 2nd Class Alvin Dvorak, Petty Officer 3rd Class Lauren Bruner, and five crewmen were in their gun director—an enclosed steel cube that controlled their antiaircraft weapons—above the bridge when their battleship exploded from the fourth bomb.

Smoke and flames raced up the side of the turret and engulfed the director. The eight men ducked behind some equipment to shield themselves, but it did little good. Intense heat momentarily sucked out the air, and flames burned away the men's clothes, scorched their skin, and melted their hair. They nearly passed out from the pain and the heat.

In a panic, two men jumped out and were never seen alive again. The survivors in the director were in agony as they huddled together, too stunned to move. Moments later, when the tall flames began to recede, a slight sea breeze blew away the smoke in front of the men. Barely able to stand, they stepped out of the director and onto a smoldering platform way too hot to lie or sit on. The heat was melting the soles of their shoes. Everything around the six sailors was glowing red-hot as the ship's superstructure slowly collapsed and the flames raged below them.

"The ladders are blown away," Stratton said, raising his charred hands in despair. "There's no way down."

Then he looked across the way at the *Vestal* and saw crewmen chopping the hawsers that had been securing the repair ship to the *Arizona*. Pointing to a muscular ax-wielding seaman on the *Vestal* who was closest to the trapped men, Stratton said, "He's our only hope."

Dvorak, who was severely burned and in excruciating pain, shouted and waved at the *Vestal* sailor. "Help! Help! Over here!" he yelled.

On the *Vestal*, Joe George, the navy boxing champ, had just raised his ax to take his first whack at a hawser when he heard the cries for help. Seeing the six *Arizona* sailors stranded on the antiaircraft gun-control platform, he knew it was impossible for them to escape on their own.

"George!" hollered an ensign behind him. "Cut that line! Pronto!"

In all his years in the navy, George had never disobeyed an order. But his heart told him this was one time when he simply must. He just couldn't carry out the officer's command and allow six men to burn alive. No, he had to help them. And he knew exactly how to do it.

George dropped his ax and picked up a nearby heaving line. The lightweight line, which had a weight on the free end, was designed to be thrown from one ship to another. He reared back and flung the heaving line over the burning water and up to the gun-control platform.

Stratton, Bruner, and Dvorak caught it. Then George tied his end of the heaving line to a much heavier rope—a line he hoped would save their lives. Despite their pain, the trapped sailors began pulling the heavy line across the water until they could tie it off on a strong part of the platform.

When George saw that they had secured their end, he did the same thing on his end. Once again, he heard the ensign holler, "George! We need to get out of here right now! Cut the line! That's a direct order from the captain!"

George shook his head and pointed to the six sailors. "We can't let them die!" he shouted back.

On the *Arizona's* gun-control platform, Dvorak, weak and in agony, muttered, "I don't know if I can make it across."

"You have to," said Stratton. "It's our only way out."

"Okay," said Dvorak. "But let me go last. I don't want to slow the rest of you."

Seaman 1st Class Harold Kuhn went first, followed by Seaman 1st Class Russell Lott, Gunner's Mate 1st Class Earl Riner, then Stratton, Bruner, and Dvorak. Hand over burned hand, the men worked their way toward the *Vestal*. Ignoring the pain from their singed, peeling palms, they dangled 40 feet in the air on their perilous journey through the smoke belching from the burning deck and over the flaming water that separated the two ships.

Stratton, 19, chose not to look down. *One hand at a time,* he told himself. *One hand at a time. Lord, we could use a little help, please.* Stratton took a quick glance at the three sailors ahead of him. *They're almost there. Good.* Seeing them gave him confidence that he, too, could make it to safety.

But when he was 20 feet from the *Vestal*, Stratton hesitated. The stinging pain in his hands and in his arm muscles were almost too much to bear. He had grown weaker.

George, who had a strong grip on the line even though it was secured, shouted to Stratton, "Come on, kid! You can do it!"

Grunting and wincing, Stratton finally reached the *Vestal*, where he collapsed in a heap on the deck. He was greeted by the three sailors who had gone ahead of him. Then he joined them in cheering on Bruner and Dvorak, who also made it safely across.

"That was quite a feat," Stratton said, "considering all the skin came off of our hands."

Before being put aboard a small boat to shore where a truck would transport them to the naval hospital, the men thanked George. "Without you, we would have fried up there," Stratton told him. "You saved our lives."

George shrugged and said, "You would have done the same if the situation were reversed."

At 8:45 A.M., the last of the mooring lines to the *Arizona* were cut. A tug showed up just in time to pull the *Vestal's* bow away from the burning battleship. The tug's captain, who had served aboard the repair ship a few months earlier, gave Young the thumbs-up sign as the damaged repair ship chugged out into the harbor. But the *Vestal* was slowly listing to starboard and settling by the stern from the water pouring in from the hole in her hull.

At 9:10 A.M., shortly after a second wave of enemy planes attacked Pearl Harbor, the *Vestal* anchored in 35 feet of water off McGrew Point about a mile away from the *Arizona*. Hampered by a lack of water caused by busted pipes, sailors were having great difficulty trying to put out the stubborn fires that were still burning on her deck. Down below, crewmen couldn't contain the water that was flowing into her aft compartments.

"Sir, the ship is sinking," Hesser told Young after receiving the latest damage reports.

"I know," the captain replied. "She's in an unstable condition, and the Japs are attacking again. The only way to save her is to beach her."

Studying a chart of the harbor, he pointed to a shallow area called Aiea Bay and said, "We'll ground her here on Aiea Shoal. It'll prevent her from sinking, and she won't be blocking a vital part of the harbor."

At 9:50 A.M., the *Vestal* got under way again and beached herself a few hundred yards away on a shallow reef.

"Well done, sir," Hesser told Young. "You saved the ship."

The captain nodded and vowed, "The *Vestal* will sail again."

Seven Vestal *crewmen died and 19 were hospitalized from the attack.*

During the following week, the Vestal's *seamen worked on repairing their own ship. They pumped out the oil and water that had flooded the compartments and then patched the hole in the hull. She eventually was towed to a dry dock, where they completed repairs, and by February 18—only ten weeks after the attack—the* Vestal *was seaworthy once again.*

That same month, Cassin Young was promoted to captain and also awarded the Medal of Honor for his gritty determination and courageous actions to save his ship. In that same ceremony, Lionel Baker received the Navy Cross for his "heroic conduct in treating wounded shipmates while under heavy machine-gun fire at Pearl Harbor."

In July 1942, Young was given command of the heavy cruiser USS San Francisco. Four months later, on the morning of November 12, 20 Japanese warships were sighted off the coast of Guadalcanal, a vitally strategic island held by US Marines northeast of Australia. Young led the outnumbered thirteen-ship American force in a fierce two-day, close-in sea battle that ultimately prevented the Japanese from retaking the island—a triumph that President Franklin Roosevelt called "the turning point in the war." But during the fight, a shell fired by the Japanese battleship Hiei slammed into the bridge of the San Francisco, killing the captain. For his brave actions that day, Young, who was buried at sea, was posthumously awarded the Navy Cross. In addition, a new destroyer was named after him.

The Vestal served valiantly throughout the war, performing thousands of vital repairs—often under dangerous conditions—on hundreds of American ships.

Joe George did not receive any medal for his efforts in saving the lives of the six Arizona seamen. (Alvin Dvorak died from his burns on Christmas Eve, 17 days after the attack). Believing that George was a hero, some of the survivors lobbied the navy to give him a medal, but officials balked, partly because he disobeyed a direct order. "He should have the Navy Cross," Stratton said in 2014. "He saved six people's lives. He refused to cut the line no matter what." Stratton, who was hospitalized for more than a year for burns covering over 60 percent of his body, said survivors of the

Arizona *had planned to honor George at one of their functions, but George died before the invitation was sent.*

In 2003, the ashes of Russell Lott were interred in the wreck-age of the Arizona. *The following year, the ashes of Paul Urdzik were scattered with full military honors at the spot where the* Vestal *had been moored next to the* Arizona.

THE TOMB AND THE SANCTUARY

Heroes of the USS *Oklahoma* and the
Navy Yard's Shop 11

General quarters! General quarters! All hands, man your battle stations!"

Within seconds, the battleship USS *Oklahoma* was rocked by a blast from a torpedo that slammed into the port side just below the waterline. Over the loudspeaker, a boatswain shouted, "This *really* is a Japanese air attack! No kidding!" Seconds later, two more torpedoes dropped from enemy planes struck the *Oklahoma* in nearly the same place, triggering explosions that ripped open a 70-foot gash through the five-inch-thick steel hull.

Above the clanging, gonging alarm bells, sailors hollered, "Another fish [torpedo] is coming our way!" The ship shuddered from a fourth explosion.

The attack couldn't have come at a worse time. Because of an upcoming admiral's inspection, the portholes, hatches, and watertight doors had been left open to air them out. Water easily gushed in and began flooding the ship's compartments, causing the vessel to lurch to port.

Everything that wasn't fastened down slid across the decks. Dishes and glasses fell off shelves and shattered. Stored ammunition and shells for the large guns rolled along the floor. The *Oklahoma* continued to list until it was almost impossible for anyone to stand up without grabbing hold of a railing. Within minutes, the order was given to abandon ship.

And then it capsized.

As the vessel rolled on her side, the sailors who were topside leaped overboard into the oil-burning water. Some were strafed by swooping Japanese fighter planes. Those seamen who weren't hit by bullets swam over to the battleship USS *Maryland*, which was moored next to the *Oklahoma*. They climbed aboard and joined her crew in manning the antiaircraft batteries.

At the time of the first torpedo blast, Ensign John England, who was looking forward to celebrating his twenty-first birthday in four days, was in one of the radio rooms belowdecks. He bolted up to the main deck to see what was happening. But rather than abandon ship as she was slowly capsizing, he dashed back to the radio room, where several sailors lay wounded. England carried a bleeding seaman to the main deck and then returned two more times to bring out injured crewmen. Even though he knew the vessel was overturning, he once again charged belowdecks for the fourth time in an attempt to rescue another sailor. England was never seen again.

Because the *Oklahoma* had suffered so much damage, she lost all power, plunging the interior into darkness. Another explosion—the fifth direct hit from a torpedo—finished her off. In less than 20 minutes, the capsized ship hit bottom in the harbor's shallow water. The stricken 583-foot-long, 30,800-ton vessel settled on her port side, exposing a third of the starboard hull and one of her giant brass propellers. The rest of the ship lay underwater. Only the 125-foot-tall masts of the superstructure that dug into the muddy bottom kept the vessel from turning completely over.

Inside the *Oklahoma*, more than 400 sailors were now facing a watery death. Many were gasping for air, searching for air pockets, or trying to orient themselves to a frightening upside-down world. Among those trapped was the ship's chaplain, Lieutenant Junior Grade Aloysius Schmitt, a Catholic priest serving his first tour of duty at sea. He had just finished celebrating Mass when the Japanese struck. As one torpedo after another devastated the ship, Father Schmitt headed toward sick bay, planning to minister to the injured and dying.

But when the ship capsized, he and eight seamen found themselves cooped up in a compartment that had one small porthole, which was facing up and the only way out. While water was rising rapidly, Father Schmitt helped each man squeeze through the porthole to safety. Only when he saw that he was the last one in the room did he take his turn. But because he was a big fellow, he couldn't quite cram his body through the porthole even after some of the men he had assisted were now on the other side grabbing his arms and trying to yank him free.

He then became aware that four more sailors had swum from an adjoining water-filled compartment and were now waiting to escape through the porthole. Knowing that he was blocking their way and time was running out before the room flooded completely, Father Schmitt told the seamen outside, "Push me back. There are others here who can get through the porthole more easily than I can."

"But you'll never get out of there alive!" one of the sailors up top told him.

"Please let go of me," the priest insisted. "More can be saved."

Reluctantly, the seamen released their grip, and he wriggled back into the rapidly flooding compartment and helped the other four seamen out through the porthole. After the final man escaped, Father Schmitt poked his head through the open porthole and told the sailors, "God bless you all." Then he disappeared under the rising murky water.

In the boiler control room, 15 sailors realized their only escape was an open hatchway that was now 8 feet above them because the ship had rolled. Water was pouring into the room when, from the compartment above, Francis Day, the ship's burly, six-foot-three, 225-pound chief water tender, appeared in the hatchway.

The 37-year-old navy veteran, who had 16 years' service under his belt, thrust his arm down the opening and hollered to the men below, "Give me your hand!" One by one, he lifted each shipmate through the hatch with a single heave. He pulled out the last man just as the boiler room filled completely with water.

Pointing to a porthole directly above them, he told them, "There's your way out." No one said anything, but they instantly knew what he knew: He was way too big to fit through the porthole. But rather than try to find another way out, he stayed and hoisted each man up so they could squirm out the porthole and then slide down the hull into the water. To the last sailor he boosted to the porthole, Day said, "Good luck, kid." Then he waited to die.

In another compartment below the third deck, Seamen 1st Class George DeLong and James Bounds, both 19 years old, and six others were cleaning up their living quarters when their life turned topsy-turvy. The series of explosions from the torpedoes had knocked them out of their bunks. As they tried to steady themselves and head for their battle stations, the ship began to roll. To their dismay, they discovered that the sailors on the deck above them had dogged (sealed) a hatch, preventing the eight seamen from climbing out.

Then the lights went out and the ship capsized. One of the men had the foresight to get a flashlight before their cramped area turned dark. The beam from the flashlight revealed that water was flowing through a two-foot-square fresh-air vent.

"Let's stuff it with clothes," Bounds suggested.

Grabbing T-shirts, pants, and jackets, the men jammed the items into the vent, but the torrent was just too strong and kept blowing out the clothes. The sailors then rolled up a bunk mattress and shoved it against the vent. Even when they took turns pressing their backs against the mattress, the water kept spurting and was now up to their chests.

Just then, a square board from a backgammon-like game called acey-deucey floated by. DeLong snared it and placed it against the vent. "Look," he said. "It's the right size to fit over the hole. How lucky is that?"

The seamen secured it over the vent with rope. Although the game board didn't completely prevent the water from coming in, it slowed the flow.

"All this did was buy us some time," said DeLong. "The compartment will still fill up with water and drown us unless we do something to get out of here."

The sailor with the flashlight pointed to a watertight door that led into a large compartment known as the aft steering room. "We could try that," he said.

"We don't know what's on the other side," an older shipmate said. "It could be full of water, and if we open it, we'll drown."

"True," said DeLong. "But if we stay here, we'll surely drown or suffocate."

"Unless we get rescued before then," said Bounds, always the optimist.

A veteran sailor responded, "Who even knows we're here? No one. Besides, we're still hearing bombs exploding outside. Maybe everyone in Pearl Harbor is dead."

"We can't stay here," DeLong contended. "We could last longer in the steering room because it's much bigger and it should have more air."

"Or more water," warned the veteran.

"Okay, let's put it to a vote," said DeLong. "Majority rules. How many want to open the door to the steering room?" After six men raised their hands, DeLong said, "Okay, let's do it and pray there's air on the other side."

With much apprehension, they opened the door. To their relief, the 40-foot-by-30-foot steering room was dry and full of air. They hustled into the room, but oily water rushed in with them and reached knee level before they could close the door.

Although the steering room was watertight, there weren't any hatches or other doorways from which to escape. The eight seamen had effectively sealed themselves from immediate danger. But now some wondered if this compartment would be their sanctuary or their tomb. With no way to exit on their own, their only chance of survival was for rescuers on top to locate them and cut them out.

After finding two wrenches, the men took turns banging SOS on the bulkhead, hoping that someone would hear them and save them before they ran out of air.

Unexpectedly, they heard a faint voice say, "Is anyone there?"

The men perked up, thinking for a brief moment that help had arrived and would soon free them from their chamber of doom. "We're here!" they shouted. "We're here in the steering room!"

But their rising spirits were crushed when the voice responded from the other side of the bulkhead, "We're trapped in an air pocket in Number Four radio room right next door to you. There are six of us. I'm Tom Hannon."

"Hey, Tom, any chance that there's a rescue effort under way?" DeLong asked.

"None that we know of," Hannon replied. "It looks bad, real bad. We're just sitting here, waiting and hoping. There's nothing else we can do."

Hannon then heard voices coming through the opposite wall. They were from another adjacent compartment known as the lucky bag room. The "lucky bag" was a large locker where misplaced clothes and other items were stowed until claimed by their owners. Yelling through the thick wall, Hannon made contact with cook Mike Savarese.

Hannon learned the lucky bag room contained 11 seamen who had ridden out the ship's rollover in the handling room under the No. 4 gun turret. When the handling room began to flood, they had moved to the lucky bag room and hunkered down there.

"Well, at least twenty-five seamen are still alive," Hannon told Savarese. "Eight in the steering room, six here in Radio Four, and you eleven in the lucky bag room."

"Knowing we're not alone doesn't cheer us up," Savarese said.

The one pressing thought on everyone's mind: *Will rescuers find us in time before we suffocate or drown?*

Julio DeCastro, a 40-year-old Hawaiian-born civilian worker at the Pearl Harbor Navy Yard, was relaxing in his house 5 miles away with his wife and 5 children, when he heard the drone of more than 100 planes. Thinking it was unusual for the military to hold flight training exercises on Sunday morning, he stepped outside, accompanied by his children. The kids smiled and waved at the planes that were now flying at treetop level over the house.

Seeing the red symbol of the rising sun on the underside of the wings, DeCastro was seized with a sickening sensation. *The war has started*, he thought. He told his family, "I have to go to the navy yard right now."

When he arrived, he gaped at the bedlam in the harbor. Swarming Japanese planes were swooping and zooming over the docks, airfields, and ships like angry hornets, releasing bombs and torpedoes and machine-gunning the men diving for cover. The USS *Arizona* was blown up and belching thick, black smoke. The *Oklahoma* was capsizing. Other ships lay crippled, listing, burning, or sinking. Then, as swiftly as the raiders attacked, they disappeared, leaving in their wake unimaginable devastation.

At around 11 A.M. DeCastro, who was supervisor of the navy yard's Shop 11, was ordered to put a team together, gather the necessary equipment, and hurry to the overturned *Oklahoma* because there were reports that hundreds of sailors were trapped inside and needed to be cut out of the hull. The first man he chose was his best worker, 21-year-old Hawaiian-born Joe Bulgo, a six-foot, 300-pound "chipper" who could handle a pneumatic chipping hammer better than anyone. The handheld device had a chisel on the end, much like a jackhammer, and was designed to chip off a ship's old paint and rust.

Once his 20-man team was assembled, DeCastro and the workers jumped into a launch and headed for the *Oklahoma*. On the way there, the men hardly said a word as their boat motored in oil-slick waters past floating bodies and twisted wreckage and through clouds of acrid smoke from enormous flames engulfing the superstructures of once proud ships.

When the Shop 11 workers neared the capsized *Oklahoma*, she reminded them of a beached gray whale lying on its side. After climbing onto the exposed starboard side of the hull, the men were met by an officer who was studying blueprints of the ship. The hull was made from huge sheets of steel riveted together in rows known as frames. In between many of the frames were large fuel, water, and sewage tanks separated by three- to six-foot-wide empty spaces called voids. With the help of the blueprints, the officer was trying to figure out the best places on the hull for rescuers to cut into so they could gain access inside.

"We don't know how many men are still alive and trapped below—maybe dozens, maybe hundreds," the officer told DeCastro. "We're hearing faint tapping sounds and even shouts coming from various areas of the ship. Mainly it's SOS. But sounds echo throughout the hull, so we aren't exactly sure where the men are holed up."

A rescue team from another ship had tried to cut a hole using an acetylene torch to free two sailors trapped in a cork-lined compartment. But the effort turned disastrous. The heat from the torch ignited the cork, creating poisonous fumes and consuming the oxygen. When rescuers finally broke into the compartment, they discovered the sailors had died from suffocation.

Even though using acetylene torches was the fastest and easiest way to cut steel, it was just too dangerous for the survivors. That's why DeCastro and his team were brought in. They were experts at using the slower, more cumbersome chipping equipment. Even though their pneumatic hammers weren't specifically designed for cutting, especially through the hull's five-inch-thick steel, the tools could eventually punch out holes with chipping blades.

So DeCastro and Bulgo—the team's two strongest chippers—and their fellow workers began the task of breaking into the hull with their pneumatic hammers, which were powered by compressed air flowing through hoses connected to the nearby battleship USS *Tennessee*. As the hammers pounded the steel, the workers' muscles throbbed to the vibrations, and their ears turned numb from the constant, earsplitting racket.

In the pitch-black lucky bag room, oxygen was slowly leaking out of the air pocket, and the water was rising at a matching pace. Seaman 1st Class Steve Young figured it would be only a matter of time before they died.

"Hey, Wimpy," he whispered to his shipmate, Seaman 1st Class Wilbur "Wimpy" Hinsperger. "I'll bet you a dollar we'll suffocate before we'll drown."

"I'll take that bet," Hinsperger said. "I think we'll drown first."

Why do I have to die down here like this, trapped in a sunken ship? Young thought. *Why couldn't it have been up in the sun or under the stars in the open air? Or on the deck of the ship while guns are firing? But here we are in the darkness without a chance to fight back.* Soon a different thought emerged. *Perhaps dying like this requires a different kind of courage.*

Noticing that his fists were clenched and his face was sweating, Young decided to make his peace with God. In silence he prayed, *Oh, God, relieve us of our torment. If it is your will that we die here, then please watch over my family and comfort them. If I have sinned in your eyes, then forgive me.*

The work was hard and tedious for the men from Shop 11, but they kept up a steady pace, hour after hour into the afternoon and then into the night. Even when antiaircraft guns began firing—there was a scary moment when American planes were mistaken for the enemy—the workers kept toiling away, knowing that time was critical for those whom fate held captive below. Because of concerns the Japanese might return for another attack, the workers weren't allowed to use any floodlights. Their only form of illumination came from the fires that still burned on the USS *Arizona.*

The workers kept hitting dead ends. Each hole they made was creating an increasingly dire situation—it was letting out trapped air which had been keeping the water level down inside. The more cuts being made, the higher the water rose and the less time rescuers had to reach the trapped men before they would drown.

Around midnight, Bulgo created a new hole that held promise. Water began bubbling out, so DeCastro kneeled down and tasted it. "It's fresh water," he announced. "If we drain this fresh water tank and drill out the bottom, we'll find a way in through one of the voids."

It took several long hours for a pump to remove enough water before DeCastro, Bulgo, and several others could jump into the now empty tank. Wielding a pneumatic hammer and a drill, they cut out a hole in the bottom of the tank. Just as DeCastro thought, they had found a dry void on the other side. "This will get us in!" he said.

*   *   *

In No. 4 radio room, Tom Hannon and his five fellow sailors kept up a steady rapping on the pipes with a wrench—three quick strikes followed by three slower ones and then three quick strikes, which is Morse code for SOS. Hour after hour, they waited for a response, but none had come.

Then, unexpectedly, Hannon thought he heard a new sound—*rat-a-tat-tat*. *Am I imagining this?* he wondered. He was about to ask the others if they had heard it, too, when the noise stopped. But it started again, a little louder and more sustained.

"Are you hearing that?" Hannon asked the others.

"What is it?" asked one of the seamen.

"It sounds like a drill or a pneumatic hammer," Hannon replied. His heart started pounding with excitement. "It can only mean one thing. They're coming for us!"

The sailor who held the wrench began banging on the pipes harder.

As the hours dragged on in the aft steering room, the air in the dark compartment grew staler. The eight men, most clad only in their skivvies, remained quiet, knowing that needless talking would waste what precious little oxygen was left. Each sailor was lost in his own thoughts—mostly of death and of loved ones they might never see again. Some rummaged through their mental lists of regrets and promised themselves they would definitely do better if only given one more chance to live.

No one knew the time. What did it matter, anyway? Time would last only as long as there was air to breathe.

Bounds refused to think of death. *Somehow, some way, we're going to get out of here,* he told himself. *I just know it.* When he took his turn tapping out the SOS repeatedly, he did it with authority because he believed with every fiber in his body that they would be saved if rescuers could hear them.

Having only a small lamp to see by, DeCastro and Bulgo went into the capsized ship, trying to find the sources of the tapping. Advancing in the dim light was disorienting because the decks of the ship were now the overheads, and overheads were now decks. Opening up one bulkhead after another, the rescuers entered debris-filled compartments and passageways, but the only sailors they found were dead.

The air was heavy and hot and reeked of the sickening smell of fuel oil, waste, and death. The men kept hearing tapping, but it was nearly impossible to tell where the sounds originated because of the ship's many decks, hundreds of passageways and compartments, and miles of pipes and conduit.

Although they were discouraged, the men kept moving and searching. There was no time to rest, no time to think how weary and hungry and thirsty they were, not as long as they could still hear life, still hear the desperate knocking sounds of SOS.

Deep inside the echoing hull, Bulgo joked, "I feel like Jonah in the belly of the whale."

DeCastro chuckled, but his laugh was cut short when the ship began to groan and sway. Both men knew that if the *Oklahoma* settled farther into the harbor's bottom and completely turned turtle, they, too, would become trapped with no chance of escape. Freezing in place for a moment, the two held their breath and let pass the urge to turn around. They relaxed when the vessel stopped shifting and all was quiet again—except for three quick raps, three slower ones, three quick ones.

The pair tapped back by banging their tools against the bulkhead. And then they heard a response. "We're getting closer," DeCastro said. As they moved forward, the rapping sounds became clearer. The men stopped and listened carefully. "It's coming from below us," DeCastro said.

They lifted off a manhole cover and lowered themselves about eight feet into an empty compartment. After banging on the nearest bulkhead, they heard a responding tapping sound, only this time much louder. From the other side of the bulkhead, sailors shouted, "We're here! We're here!"

"We're going to cut you out of there," DeCastro yelled back. "It'll take some time, but you'll soon be free."

When word reached above that survivors had been located, several workers followed the air hose of Bulgo's pneumatic hammer and scurried through the void to help him and DeCastro.

Using their equipment, DeCastro and Bulgo worked feverishly over the next hour. The chiseling against steel created a deafening, screeching racket, but to the trapped men, it sounded better than a symphony orchestra. Finally, the workers broke through the bulkhead and into the No. 4 radio room. It was shortly after 6 A.M. Monday, nearly 22 hours after the *Oklahoma* had capsized.

One by one, six weary men emerged from the radio room. Hugging Bulgo, a sailor gushed, "You're a lifesaver. I could kiss you!" Another one, trembling with emotion, shook DeCastro's hand and repeated, "Thank you, thank you, thank you!"

Seeing that the rescued seamen couldn't reach the open manhole above by themselves, Bulgo bent down and said, "Climb on my back. I'll get you out." So they did.

"More men are trapped in the aft steering room and in the lucky bag room," Hannon told DeCastro. "Can you save them?"

"Don't worry," DeCastro replied. "We'll get them out."

Hearing the joyous whoops coming from the radio room, Savarese hollered from the lucky bag room, "Get us out, too!" Then the other ten seamen with him began yelling.

On the other side of the bulkhead, DeCastro told them, "Take it easy, boys. We'll get you out. First, though, we're going to drill a small hole. Is there any water in there?"

"Some," Young replied. "Go ahead and drill."

DeCastro began boring a small hole about three-quarters of an inch in diameter, causing air to escape in a hissing sound. As the air pressure decreased, the water began to rise. "Hurry up!" Young bellowed as others joined him in cries of alarm. "The water is coming up to our waists!"

"Calm down, boys," DeCastro told them. "We're moving as fast as we can."

Bulgo picked up the pneumatic hammer and began pounding at the bulkhead. The rescuers knew that every minute counted. If they didn't reach the sailors within the next few hours, it would be too late. The sailors would drown.

His arms burning from exertion, the sweat-drenched Bulgo threw his hefty weight behind the chipping hammer and made the first cut. It took about an hour.

"Hold on, boys!" DeCastro shouted. "We're making progress."

Bulgo ignored the pain in his back and limbs and pounded through the steel, creating a second slash. Another hour had gone by. He had never worked the hammer so hard and so fast in his life. Then he finished the third cut.

"The water is really getting high in here," Young reported. "It's up to our chests!"

"Stay calm," DeCastro replied. "Hold on a little longer. We're almost through. To save time, we're going to use a sledgehammer to bend the steel."

Taking a couple of deep breaths, Bulgo slammed the sledgehammer over and over against the steel plate that he had cut in three places. With each swing, the piece bent back a few inches. Again and again, Bulgo swung the sledgehammer, refusing to give his fatigued body even a few seconds of rest.

Finally, he beat out a hole big enough for a man to get

through. As water poured out of the opening, DeCastro told them, "Come out one at a time."

Savarese and Young were the first two to leave the lucky bag room. "I'm out! I'm free! I'm alive!" Young joyously roared. It was 9 A.M. The sailors had been confined in the steering room for 25 hours.

Entering the next compartment outside the radio room, Savarese pointed to the open manhole above them and said, "I don't have the strength to get up there."

"Up on my back," said Bulgo, kneeling down. Savarese hopped onto Bulgo's shoulders and then reached up toward the opening, where members of DeCastro's team gripped his wrists and pulled him out.

Some of the oil-covered sailors didn't need Bulgo's help, but the weaker ones did. He became their human ladder, letting them use his clasped hands as a step to climb onto his shoulders so that his coworkers above could haul them through the open manhole.

As the sailors popped out of a hole in the overturned hull and inhaled their first breath of fresh air since the attack, some broke down and wept. "It's a miracle!" a seamen yelled. On the *Maryland*, which had been moored alongside the *Oklahoma*, crewmen who were aware of the life-and-death drama unfolding inside the capsized ship cheered the rescued men.

Young turned to Hinsperger, grinned, and said, "Neither of us won that bet, thank God."

*   *   *

For DeCastro, Bulgo, and the rest of the valiant team from Shop 11, their work wasn't over. They needed to free the eight seamen entombed in the aft steering room—a task the workers knew would be much more difficult and time-consuming than the first two rescues. Despite not sleeping for more than a day, DeCastro and Bulgo labored tirelessly to break into the compartment. They were making steady, but slow, progress. Three hours went by. Then another three. By now, the water was rising not only in the steering room but also on the other side of the bulkhead where DeCastro and Bulgo were working. The water was up to their waists.

"When can you free us?" a seaman shouted to the pair. "We can't hang on much longer."

"Take it easy, boys," DeCastro told them in his steady, calm voice. "We're close to getting you out." Two more hours passed.

"It's filling up in here!" a seaman shouted to the rescuers.

"It's really tough to breathe," another reported.

Time definitely was running out on them. DeCastro and Bulgo knew that if they couldn't break into the steering room within the hour, they would be recovering bodies rather than saving sailors. Gritting his teeth, Bulgo willed himself—and, in a way, his chipping hammer—to work faster, harder.

Thirty minutes later, a seaman warned, "We're treading water!"

"Hold on, boys," DeCastro said. "We're almost through."

Finally, after nine grueling hours, the workers busted into the compartment with only a few minutes to spare before it would have completely filled with water and drowned the men.

"I knew it!" Bounds exclaimed as he swam out of the room. "I just *knew* we'd be rescued."

The ordeal for the eight men had lasted for thirty-six nightmarish hours. Now it was over. By the time the last sailor in the room was freed, the water was up to Bulgo's neck. After DeCastro dogged the hatch, the two of them followed the pneumatic hammer's hose line through a compartment, up into a void, and eventually out onto the hull. It was after 6 P.M. Monday, and dusk had descended over the ravaged harbor.

A launch had just pulled away, transporting the eight rescued seamen, who were wrapped in blankets, to the hospital ship USS *Solace*. Bulgo and DeCastro waved to them, but in the twilight, the sailors were too far away to see their saviors.

Worn out beyond what they thought their bodies could endure, Bulgo and DeCastro plopped down on the hull and swigged water from canteens. Any thoughts of taking a break and going home were soon quashed. From somewhere below, they once again heard the faint sounds that had consumed them for the last day and a half—three quick taps, three slower ones, three quick ones.

For the men of Shop 11, there were more lives to save.

In addition to the 25 seamen that Julio DeCastro, Joe Bulgo, and their fellow civilian workers rescued, 7 more trapped sailors were eventually pulled out alive—the last ones more than 48 hours after the Oklahoma had capsized.

Later in 1941, the navy awarded citations for "heroic work with utter disregard of personal safety" to DeCastro, Bulgo, and the 18 other workers from Shop 11.

After the war, DeCastro continued to work at the shipyard and retired in his native Hawaii. He died at the age of 83 in 1984.

Bulgo married, had four kids, and worked at the San Francisco Naval Shipyard until his retirement following two heart attacks. One of his regrets was that he never had a chance to talk with those sailors he had helped rescue.

But in 1987, journalist Mayo Simon, who had written a story about the amazing rescue efforts of the workers of Shop 11, arranged for Bulgo to attend a dinner at the annual convention of the USS Oklahoma Association in San Jose, California. Bulgo, who was confined to a wheelchair because he was suffering from terminal bone cancer, was seated at the head of the table, but no one in the audience knew who he was.

Simon was the keynote speaker at the event and recounted Bulgo's heroic efforts to free the trapped sailors. "I know three of the men he saved are here tonight," Simon told the audience. "And I also know you never got a chance to thank him. So if there's something you would like to say to that Hawaiian kid who risked his life to save yours 46 years ago—well, he's right over there."

Recalling that poignant moment at the dinner, Simon wrote, "It was impossible to describe the emotions that swept the hall as I pointed to Joe, and two hundred people rose to their feet and cheered.

He covered his face with his napkin. He didn't want them to see him crying. Three elderly veterans embraced the man who could no longer stand, even to acknowledge the applause, but on whose broad, strong back they had once been carried."

Joe Bulgo died two months later, no longer a forgotten hero.

Sadly, most of those who were aboard the ship when she was torpedoed perished. The casualty count of 429 officers and crewmen was the second-highest in the attack, exceeded only by that of the Arizona.

For their selfless actions, Father Aloysius Schmitt and Francis Day were posthumously awarded the Navy and Marine Corps Medal. Each had a destroyer escort named after him. Father Schmitt was the first American chaplain of any faith to die in World War II. After John England gave up his life to save others, the navy named two destroyer escorts in his honor.

Others on the Oklahoma who were honored posthumously for sacrificing their own lives after helping crewmen escape flooded compartments were Ensign Francis Flaherty and Seaman 1st Class James Richard Ward (the Medal of Honor for each), Chief Carpenter John Austin (Navy Cross), and Lieutenant Commander Hugh Alexander (Navy and Marine Corps Medal). For each hero, the navy named a destroyer escort after him, except Alexander.

Others who received the Navy Cross for risking their lives to save shipmates were Boatswain Adolph Bothne, Marine Private 1st Class Willard Darling, and Marine Sergeant Thomas E. Hailey.

Only 35 of those who perished on the Oklahoma were positively identified. Most of the remains were interred in mass graves at the Punchbowl Cemetery (officially known as the National Memorial Cemetery of the Pacific) in Honolulu, Hawaii.

As for the stricken ship, she was raised, decommissioned, and stripped of her guns and superstructure. In 1947, she was sold to a company for scrap metal but sank in the Pacific Ocean while being towed to Oakland, California. Although the ship served in two world wars, she never fired a single round from any of her guns in combat.

The USS Oklahoma Memorial, which was dedicated in 2007, rests on the shores of Ford Island, next to the former berth of the Oklahoma.

Stephen Bower Young, one of the 32 sailors rescued by the workers of Shop 11, wrote a book about his experience called Trapped at Pearl Harbor: Escape from Battleship Oklahoma, which was used as one of the source materials for this story.

"WE SURE BROKE UP THEIR LITTLE PARTY"

Heroes of the 47th Pursuit Squadron

Hotshot fighter pilots Ken Taylor and George Welch were living the life that most red-blooded American males in 1941 could only fantasize about. The young aviators lived on a base in sun-kissed Hawaii and spent their free hours—which were many because it was peacetime—enjoying all the blessings that the island provided: the beach parties, the dinner dances, the nightclubs, the big bands, the poker games, the bars . . . and the girls!

For Taylor and Welch, there was nowhere else in the world they would rather be. They were doing what they loved most—flying—and living in what to them was sheer paradise.

Oh, sure, Japan was rattling its sabers, but the aviators figured it was just some posturing from a smaller country on the other side of the Pacific. Nothing to worry about.

Until there was.

*   *   *

Hawaii was a far cry from where Ken Taylor grew up in a modest middle-class family in Hominy, Oklahoma. His parents taught him the importance of working hard and giving his best. An excellent student, Ken spent two years at the University of Oklahoma before enlisting in the Army Air Corps (forerunner of the US Air Force). After graduating from aviation training, he was commissioned a second lieutenant and, in the summer of 1941, was assigned to the 47th Pursuit Squadron at Wheeler Army Airfield, Hawaii's main fighter base. The squadron was tasked with protecting the navy ships at Pearl Harbor, about 12 miles away from the field.

George Welch was the son of a wealthy researcher at the DuPont chemical company in Wilmington, Delaware. George's real last name was Schwartz, but because of anti-German prejudice following the end of World War I, his parents legally changed his and his brother's last name to Welch, which was his mother's maiden name. George attended private schools, and excelled at sports more than his studies. Nicknamed "Cowboy," he was voted by his fellow students at boarding school as the senior class's laziest student. He then attended Purdue University, where he majored in mechanical engineering, but quit to join the Army Air Corps, and learned to fly. Commissioned a second lieutenant, Welch was sent to the 47th Squadron shortly before Taylor arrived there.

When they met on their dream assignment in Hawaii, the small-town hick and the rich kid hit it off right away and became best buds. They had much in common. Both were good-looking, personable, wiry men who stood about five feet nine inches tall and weighed 140 pounds. They loved to party, play cards late into the night, pull harmless pranks on their comrades, and flirt with the girls. The pair was known as fun-loving goofballs and mischief-makers who occasionally wound up in trouble with the brass. (The base commander impounded Welch's car after the pilot was caught speeding recklessly one too many times.) Taylor and Welch might have been rogues, but when it came to flying the one-man, single-engine fighter plane known as the P-40 Warhawk, they were "top guns," the best in the squadron.

On Saturday night, December 6, Taylor, a few weeks shy of his twenty-second birthday, and Welch, 23, made the rounds of the officers' clubs at Pearl Harbor's Hickam Field and Wheeler Field, dancing with the island's most eligible young ladies. Because the clubs required officers to wear formal attire on Saturday nights, the pilots were dressed in tuxedos. After partying until the wee hours, the two joined fellow officers in an all-night poker game.

Just as dawn was breaking, Taylor and Welch retired to their respective rooms at Wheeler's bachelor officers' quarters. Because Sunday was a duty-free day, they were looking forward to sleeping late. But, at 7:55 A.M., less than two hours after their heads hit their pillows, they were jolted awake by the sounds of explosions and machine gun fire. Donning the tuxedo pants and shirt he had worn the night before, Taylor dashed out of his room and met Welch, who was dressed the same way, in the hallway. "What's happening?" Taylor asked.

"An accident?" Welch wondered.

When they hurried outside, they saw two-man dive-bombers strafing the rows of more than 100 planes that were neatly lined up on the field. Spotting the Japanese symbol on the bomber wings, Welch blurted, "See the red meatballs? It's the Japs! They're attacking us!"

The raiders were flying just 20 to 30 feet above the ground, firing at will. The rear gunners were aiming for crewmen and officers, who were sprinting in all directions.

"We need to get to our planes," Taylor said.

The 47th Squadron's planes were at the Haleiwa Emergency Landing Field, a sandy strip about ten miles northwest of Wheeler Field. The aircraft had been moved there for a week of gunnery practice.

Pulling the keys to his Buick out of his pocket, Taylor tossed them to Welch and said, "Go get my car and bring it around to the club. I'll call Haleiwa and tell them to get our planes ready." When Taylor phoned the landing strip, he shouted, "Fuel and arm two P-40s! The Japs are here—and it's no gag!"

As enemy planes streaked overhead, firing their machine guns and dropping bombs, the two fighter pilots roared toward Haleiwa on a winding road at speeds sometimes approaching 100 miles an hour. When the pair arrived, they sprinted to their planes, which the ground crews had readied.

Getting Taylor harnessed into the cockpit, the crew chief said that the plane's two .50-caliber machine guns weren't armed because the field didn't have any ammo for them, but the four smaller .30-caliber weapons mounted on the wings were armed.

Welch learned the same thing from his crew chief, Staff Sergeant Cecil Goodroe, who added, "Lieutenant, we've received orders that the planes here are supposed to be dispersed [spread out] on the ground."

"I don't care," Welch snapped. "We're fighter pilots and that's what we intend to do—fight. Now get off my wing. I'm taking off."

Acting on their own and not bothering with any orders, Taylor and Welch put on their soft helmets, goggles, and earphones, shoved their throttles to full power, and lifted off at 8:30 A.M. They flew over besieged Wheeler Field, but by the time the pair arrived, the Japanese had departed, leaving several hangars and buildings in ruins and destroying or damaging many of the parked planes.

The 2 pilots climbed to 8,000 feet and began searching for enemy aircraft. They soon spotted 12 Japanese dive-bombers about 1,000 feet below them, strafing Ewa Field, a landing strip used by the Marines near Pearl Harbor. The enemy planes were in an echelon formation—two parallel rows, with one extending forward of the other.

Even though Taylor and Welch were outnumbered six to

one, they didn't think twice about striking back. "Let's go get them," Welch said.

Flying side by side, they dived behind the formation and began firing their machine guns, surprising the Japanese pilots. The rear gunner of a dive-bomber was so intent on strafing the airfield he never looked behind him. Welch fired a burst and watched the plane explode before falling away in chunks of debris.

Seconds later, Taylor unleashed his bullets on a dive-bomber. It erupted in flames, rolled over, and crashed near the airfield.

"First crack out of the box, and we each get a kill!" Welch radioed his comrade.

As the Japanese separated from their formation and flew off in different directions, Taylor radioed back, "Well, we sure broke up their little party, didn't we?"

The pilots gave chase to the fleeing enemy. Welch caught up with one plane and engaged in a dogfight that tested his nerve. An incendiary bullet that struck his Warhawk started a small fire behind his seat. He kept flying with one hand while successfully smothering the flames with his other gloved hand.

Banking into another attack, his P-40 took several more big hits. Bullets struck his engine, propeller, and cowling, forcing Welch to break away from the enemy so he could test the Warhawk's ability to continue the fight. To his relief, the plane was still airworthy.

Rolling out into a dive, Welch fired at point-blank range on another enemy plane and watched his second kill plunge to the ground. His bullets peppered several more aircraft, causing them to smoke, but they kept flying. Then one of his guns jammed. Discovering that his other weapons were nearly out of ammo, he turned for Wheeler Field and faced a new, troublesome concern. Few of the gunners of the antiaircraft weapons there were well trained in recognizing American planes from enemy aircraft. *I could get shot down by friendly fire,* he thought. But he landed safely without the gunners shooting at him.

Meanwhile, Taylor noticed a lone two-man dive-bomber heading out to sea, so he climbed slightly above it and then came in for the kill. His guns blazing, he shot the rear gunner but couldn't bring down the plane before it slipped behind a cloud. He continued the pursuit. As the enemy plane emerged from the cloud, it was trailing smoke and losing altitude. With great satisfaction, Taylor watched it splash into the water and break apart.

Spotting another dive-bomber trying to get away, he flew after it, and when he was close enough, he fired at its tail. Small parts of the plane broke off and it began smoking, but it still remained in the air. Closing in on it again, Taylor thought, *I've got you in my crosshairs.* But when he squeezed the trigger, nothing happened. *Damn! I'm out of ammo!* He turned around and headed for Wheeler Field to rearm.

By the time Taylor landed, Wheeler Field was in chaos. Men were fighting fires, tending to the wounded, and pushing planes out of the way to various revetments of earth and sand-bags spread throughout the base. Taylor taxied over to where Welch's plane was being armed and prepped near a hangar that hadn't been bombed—a stroke of good luck because it was full of ammunition.

From the cockpit, Taylor told a member of the ground crew, "I'm tapped out. I need the .30 cals and the .50 cals loaded up."

The crewman hesitated. "Uh, sir, I've been told to tell you to get out of the plane so it can be dispersed for safety reasons."

Overhearing the conversation, Welch shouted to Taylor, "They told me the same baloney. Ignore them, get armed, and let's get back in the air."

Turning to the crewman, Taylor barked, "Get my plane ready, now!"

The armament crew brought out a dolly that carried the ammunition for the machine guns. While the plane was being rearmed, two officers climbed onto the wing and were offering advice to Taylor about the best way to fight the Japanese. Suddenly, they heard an ominous drone. Everyone looked in the sky and saw 15 enemy planes roaring toward Wheeler Field from Pearl Harbor.

"They're gonna attack us again!" an officer shouted.

Welch yelled for everyone to move away from his plane.

"But, sir," said a crewman who had been working on the jammed .30-caliber machine gun. "I haven't been able to clear your weapon."

"I can't worry about that now," Welch snapped. "I'm taking off." Hollering to Taylor, he said, "Kenny, I'll see you upstairs!" Welch revved his engine and took off directly toward the enemy. Going the opposite way, with his tail to the Japanese, would have made him an easy target on his liftoff.

The officers who had been talking to Taylor, and the crewmen who had been servicing his plane, scrammed in search of cover from the impending strafing assault. Sitting in the cockpit alone, Taylor thought, *It's too late for me to run.* In their haste, the crew had left several ammo boxes on the wings and the armament dolly in front of the plane, but that didn't slow him. He simply gave his Warhawk the throttle, and as the ammo boxes slid off the wings, the plane jumped over the dolly without any damage.

Seeing the Japanese echelon descending on Wheeler Field, he thought, *I couldn't have timed this any better.* As he rolled down the grass runway head-on toward the enemy planes, which were coming in low, he raised the nose of his plane and began firing at them. *There's no way they can shoot at me without them flying into the ground,* he told himself. He kept the tail wheel on the ground as long as he could on his takeoff run while sending bullets ripping into several planes as they passed overhead. But he was disappointed that none was seriously damaged.

Once he was airborne, Taylor whipped his P-40 around so that he was behind what he thought was the last plane in the echelon. "You're mine," he said, squeezing the trigger. Just then, his plane shuddered from a torrent of bullets. Several bore through the canopy and lodged in the back of his seat right behind his head. Another bullet, however, pierced his arm, striking the trim-tab control on the instrument panel and sending shrapnel slicing into his leg.

Grimacing in pain, Taylor wondered, *What's happening?* Swiveling his head in all directions, he realized he had made a terrible miscalculation. He wasn't behind the echelon as he had thought. Because smoke and clouds had obscured his vision, he didn't realize until this moment that he was actually in the middle of the enemy formation.

Seeing his pal's predicament, Welch radioed, "Kenny, you have a Zero on your tail!"

"No kidding," replied Taylor.

Turning his Warhawk sharply, Welch radioed, "I'll be right there."

For the first time as a pilot, Taylor was worried. Up until this moment, he hadn't been fired on and was feeling pretty confident. He had convinced himself that aerial combat wasn't all that difficult. Now he was imperiled and injured and scared. The wave of fear was so powerful that it completely suppressed the pain from his wounds.

But that terror diminished quickly when his training kicked in. He dipped, climbed, and turned, trying to shake off his attacker.

Seconds later, Welch lined up behind Taylor's attacker. With a few quick spurts from his .50 caliber, Welch blasted it out of the sky.

"Thanks, George," Taylor said. "I owe you."

Although Taylor's plane was damaged, it was still able to fly. And so was he, despite his bloody injuries. While Welch engaged in a dogfight with another Zero, Taylor climbed above the echelon and studied it until he was sure he could locate the actual end of the formation. Then he swooped in on the trailing dive-bomber and fired away. The plane wobbled and belched heavy smoke before spinning downward and crashing into the ground for Taylor's second kill.

Taylor and Welch then broke up the echelon and drove the Japanese away from Wheeler Field. Welch chased a lone dive-bomber as it sped out to sea. The rear gunner was either dead or asleep because he was slumped over and made no effort to shoot at the American. A five-second spurt from Welch's guns was all it took for him to claim his fourth kill of the day.

Taylor pursued a dive-bomber, too, but wasn't able to score enough direct hits to bring it down. Eventually, he ran out of ammo again and returned to Haleiwa, where he was treated for his wounds. Welch, who was unscathed, fueled up and went up for the third time.

During the Japanese raid, more than a dozen Army Air Corps pilots got into the air and engaged the enemy. One of them, Second Lieutenant Philip Rasmussen, was rousted out of bed by the strafing at Wheeler Field. Still in his purple pajamas, he dashed outside and, while dodging gunfire, hopped into one of the few parked P-36 Hawks that hadn't been damaged by the attackers. Minutes earlier, his roommate, Second Lieutenant Gordon Sterling, climbed into a Hawk. With an obvious feeling of doom, Sterling took off his watch, handed it to his crew chief, and said, "Give this to my mother. I'm not coming back."

At 8:50 A.M., they took off with two other Hawks, piloted by First Lieutenant Lewis Sanders and Second Lieutenant John Thacker. After climbing to 9,000 feet, the four pilots spotted a formation of six enemy dive-bombers attacking the naval air station at Kaneohe. The Americans went after the Japanese aircraft. Sanders was the first in his group to score a victory, sending an enemy plane spiraling into the water off the coast.

Moments later, Sterling was diving after a plane high above the coastline. But at the same time, a Japanese aircraft was on Sterling's tail, firing away. Seeing his fellow airman in trouble, Sanders zoomed down to help out and maneuvered behind the plane that was shooting at Sterling. All four aircraft were aligned in a steep dive, each one, except the first, opening fire on the aircraft in front of it.

The Japanese plane that Sterling was chasing began smoking from his bullets and disappeared into a cloud. But Sterling's plane was shot up from behind, causing him to plunge into the water. The third plane, the one that knocked out Sterling's, took several bullets from Sanders's guns and began smoking. It vanished behind a cloud.

Seeing Sterling's plane splash, Rasmussen circled over it. He watched helplessly as Sterling struggled, but failed, to get out of his sinking Hawk and drowned.

Rasmussen couldn't help but think about the letter that Sterling had written a few weeks earlier and had shown him before mailing it. In it, Sterling told his parents, "Phil and I have decided that if either of us has to crash, we'll do it where they can pick us up so that the other can bring us home. That's a good arrangement, except it's more likely to be Phil that brings me home." (Sadly, Sterling's body was not recoverable.)

Shelving his thoughts about his roomie, Rasmussen rejoined Sanders and Thacker in their continuing assault on the raiders. But soon his machine guns started malfunctioning and firing on their own. While he was trying to fix the weapons, a Zero passed in front of him. Flying directly into his line of fire, the Zero was struck multiple times by Rasmussen's runaway guns and exploded in midair.

Thacker tangled with the remaining enemy aircraft, two Zeros, until all his guns jammed. He bravely continued making several passes at them while trying to clear his weapons, but to no avail. When the Japanese pilots realized he couldn't shoot, they attacked Thacker and hit his plane several times. He sought cover in the clouds and then brought his bullet-riddled aircraft back to base.

The Zeros next went after Rasmussen. He shook one of them off his tail, but the other sprayed his Hawk with bullets, shattering the canopy and severing the hydraulic lines. Rasmussen's plane began tumbling wildly for thousands of feet as he desperately fought to regain control. Somehow he halted his crippled aircraft from its death plunge and, through sheer flying skill, coaxed it back to Wheeler Field, where he landed without any brakes, rudder, or tail wheel.

Only after Rasmussen got out of the plane and examined it did he see how incredibly lucky he was. He counted nearly 500 bullet holes in the fuselage and wings. Two cannon rounds fired from the Zero were found wedged in a radio directly behind his seat. "If that radio hadn't been there, I'd have been killed," he told his ground crew.

Sanders found himself alone in the skies going against two Zeros, which were faster and more nimble than his P-36. He broke off the one-sided battle and returned to base safely.

About 30 minutes earlier, 2 planes from Bellows Field tried to join the fray but were ambushed by enemy planes. The Hawk flown by Second Lieutenant George Whiteman was hit as he cleared the ground and crashed in flames at the end of the runway, killing him instantly. A Hawk flown by First Lieutenant Sam Bishop reached 500 feet, when it burst into flames from a Zero's machine gun fire. He crashed in the water just off the coast. Although he was wounded, Bishop wriggled out of the cockpit before his aircraft sank, and he swam to shore.

While all this action was unfolding, pilots were arriving at Haleiwa by car and jumping into any plane that was ready to fight. Lieutenants Harry Brown, Robert Rogers, John Webster, and John Dains took off from the landing strip and quickly engaged the enemy. From Wheeler Field, Lieutenants Malcolm Moore and Othneil Norris also entered the air battle, in planes that were undamaged because smoke from the burning hangars had hidden them from the enemy.

Within minutes of being airborne, Rogers attacked a Zero. When he last saw it, the Zero was losing altitude and trailing black smoke as it disappeared into a cloud bank. But then Rogers was assaulted by two Zeros, so Brown swung over and shot one down and drove off the other. Judging from the smoke pouring out of several enemy aircraft, Brown and his fellow aviators had severely damaged, and possibly shot down, more planes than they could confirm.

Peeling off from the others, Webster encountered two Japanese aircraft. Less than an hour earlier, when the raid began, he had grabbed a rifle and boxes of ammunition and, from the ground, kept firing at the enemy during the first strafing run at Wheeler Field. Now he was shooting at them from the air near Haleiwa. Even though he was outnumbered, Webster kept on the attack until enemy machine gun fire tore into his plane, shattering his controls and ripping open his leg. Even with his injury and the plane's damage, he made it back safely to Haleiwa.

Dains returned to Wheeler to refuel and rearm his P-40 Warhawk and then went back into battle, where he gunned down a Zero over the Kaawa radar station on the east side of Oahu. But then another Zero shot up his plane, so he flew back to Wheeler. Finding an unattended P-36, Dains went up for a third time, joining Welch to look for more Japanese aircraft. They didn't find any because, by this time, the enemy planes were already returning to their respective aircraft carriers far out to sea.

After an hour's search, Welch and Dains turned toward Wheeler. At Schofield Barracks next to the base, gunners manning antiaircraft weapons were so unnerved by the deadly attack and so fearful of another assault that when they spotted the two planes approaching the field, the men didn't wait to identify the aircraft. They panicked and opened fire on them. Welch avoided the flak and landed safely, but Dains's plane was struck. It crashed, killing the pilot in the corps's first friendly-fire tragedy of the war.

After the injured Taylor drove from Haleiwa to Wheeler, he met up with Welch. They pounded each other on the back, grateful for their survival and proud of their victories. Wanting to see the wreckage of one of their kills, they drove off in Taylor's car. Along the way, they were stopped by Major Gordon Austin, the squadron commander. He had just returned from a duck-hunting trip on the island of Molokai and was upset that he hadn't been at the base during the attack.

Seeing the pilots in their tuxedos and knowing of their reputations as scoundrels, he assumed the worst. Already stressed by the raid, Austin, who was unaware of the pair's heroic exploits, read them the riot act. He called them "ne'er-do-wells" who shirked their duties because all they cared about was "gallivanting around the island." The spitting-mad major ended his tongue lashing by bellowing, "Now get back to Haleiwa. Don't you know there's a war going on?"

Finally able to speak, Taylor and Welch told him, in great detail, about their valiant feats in the air. Austin's face, which had been warped in anger, quickly softened and now sported a big grin. He shook their hands and, as if his ranting and raving never happened, told them, "I always said you were my two best pilots."

The 14 American pilots who engaged the enemy during the surprise attack downed at least 10 of the 29 Japanese aircraft that were lost. (Antiaircraft fire claimed 15 kills.) Air corps records credit George Welch with four kills and Ken Taylor with two, although Japanese combat reports indicate that Taylor had four kills.

Of the estimated 400 American planes on Hawaii at the time, 188 were destroyed (including 3 that were shot down) and another 159 were severely damaged (including 4 that were involved in dogfights).

Among those pilots earning a Silver Star—the military's third-highest award for valor—were Sam Bishop, Harry Brown, Malcolm Moore, Philip Rasmussen, Robert Rogers, Lewis Sanders, John Thacker, and John Webster, along with John Dains and George Whiteman (both posthumously).

General Henry "Hap" Arnold, chief of the Army Air Corps, wanted to nominate Taylor and Welch for the Medal of Honor, but he was overruled by higher-ups, allegedly because the pilots had taken off without authorization. However, a month after the Pearl Harbor attacks, the two were awarded the Distinguished Service Cross—the air corps's highest combat honor.

As a pilot during World War II, Welch, who rose to the rank of major, went on 348 missions. He became one of the corps' top aces, credited with shooting down 16 enemy aircraft. (It's believed he downed several more, but they couldn't be officially confirmed.) His combat days ended after he contracted malaria in 1943 and was hospitalized for several months in Australia. After the war, Welch became the chief test pilot for North American Aviation and was one of the first men to break the sound barrier. He was killed in 1954 during a test flight when the new fighter jet he was piloting disintegrated in midair.

Taylor, who also became a major, flew combat missions in the South Pacific, where he was credited with downing one Japanese aircraft and an additional four more that were considered "probable" kills. During an air raid at a base in Guadalcanal, he broke his leg. He returned to the United States, where he trained pilots for combat in Europe. After the war, when the corps transitioned into the US Air Force, Taylor commanded the military branch's first squadron of combat jets. He spent 27 years on active duty, retiring as a colonel. He later became a brigadier general in the Alaska Air National Guard and then worked in the insurance industry until 1985. He died in 2006 at the age of 86. He is buried in Arlington National Cemetery, as is Welch.

In 1991, at a fiftieth anniversary symposium of the Pearl

Harbor attack, Taylor met and shook hands with Zenji Abe, a former Japanese pilot who took part in the raid. "I was impressed by Mr. Taylor's grit to storm into the pack of Japanese fighters," Abe told the press. Taylor later said, "I have no hatred against Japanese people, but I do against those who started the war."

THE SHIP THAT COULDN'T BE SUNK

Heroes of the USS Nevada

The carnage along Battleship Row was overwhelming. The USS *Arizona* and USS *West Virginia* were completely engulfed in flames and sinking. The USS *Oklahoma* and USS *Utah* had capsized. Smoke was rising on the USS *Maryland*, USS *Tennessee*, and USS *Pennsylvania*, which were still under fierce attack from nonstop bombing and strafing.

The USS *Nevada*, moored last in the line of the big warships, faced almost certain destruction, too. She was listing from a torpedo that had sliced open a huge gash on her port side. Bombs were falling all around her and bullets were pounding into her decks. Fires were erupting onboard. Crewmen lay dead or dying. And a flaming oil slick from the devastated *Arizona*, which was moored in front of her, was threatening to consume her.

The *Nevada*'s gunnery crews were putting up a valiant defense, but the Japanese were relentless. Any attempt by the ship to escape seemed out of the question. She was badly damaged. The four tugboats and a civilian harbor pilot who were needed to guide her through the tricky confines of the port were under siege and unavailable. Her skipper and senior officers were not onboard. In fact, only junior officers were in charge of the ship at the moment. And the ranking officer, Lieutenant Commander Francis Thomas, was only a reservist who just months earlier was working as an industrial engineer for a steel plant in Buffalo, New York.

Given those daunting circumstances, Thomas decided there was only one way to save the ship. Even though he had no experience handling a battleship, he announced to his crew, "We're going to make a run for the open sea."

Normally, for a battleship the size of the *Nevada*, it would take more than two hours for the boilers to heat up and provide enough power for the vessel to move out. But earlier that morning, Ensign Joseph Taussig, Jr., had the foresight to order the firing up of two boilers—enough to get the ship under way within thirty minutes, but at a slow speed.

As the attack intensified, Thomas was multitasking from central station—the ship's communications center—in the belly of the vessel. Despite being under crushing pressure, he was coolly supervising preparations to get under way. At the same time, he was dispatching firefighting teams and handling counterflooding measures (flooding compartments on the opposite side of the list to balance the ship).

He had no contact with the ship's captain, Francis Scanland, or executive officer, Lieutenant Commander Lawrence Ruff, or other senior officers because none were aboard. Scanland had spent Saturday night with his family—the first time ever that he hadn't stayed overnight aboard his ship—so he could visit with his wife, daughter, and grandchildren, who had arrived in Hawaii a few days earlier. It was the first time he had met his young grandkids. Ruff was attending Catholic Mass on the hospital ship USS *Solace* when the attack began. The rest of the senior officers had been enjoying liberty in Honolulu.

Although Thomas, 37, was a reservist, he had graduated from the US Naval Academy and had experience at sea. He had left the navy for a career in the steel business, but remained in the navy reserve until he was unexpectedly called up for active duty earlier in the year. Now he found himself in command of a ship in the opening minutes of a new war.

His decision to move out was buoyed by knowing he could count on three veteran shipmates—Chief Boatswain's Mate Edwin Hill, Quartermaster Chief Robert Sedberry, and Warrant Machinist Donald Ross.

The 47-year-old Hill was a big, bald-headed man who was one of the oldest persons onboard the ship. Ever since he'd enlisted as a teenager following the death of his mother, he was all navy. Walking ramrod straight, he commanded respect and admiration from everyone who met him. He was a no-nonsense man known simply as Mister Hill, with an emphasis on the "Mister." If someone wasn't moving fast enough, Hill would growl, "Today, sailor, today!" Yet, for all his gruffness, he cared deeply about every member of the crew, and they cared deeply about him.

In the first minutes of the attack, Hill grabbed a machete and cut the ropes that were holding up awnings over the guns along the deck so they could return fire. When the torpedo blast knocked out the electric elevators that supplied ammunition to the guns on the port side, Hill immediately organized a chain of sailors who began passing the ammo hand to hand from belowdecks.

High up in the wheelhouse, Sedberry, 31, was making the necessary preparations to cast off. Almost all of his 14 years in the navy had been served on the *Nevada,* so he knew her every rivet and bolt. He possessed more experience behind the helm than all the senior officers combined—and they were the first to admit that no one could handle the ship better than the quiet, unassuming North Carolinian.

Someone from the engine room told Sedberry through the phone, "With only two boilers fired up, it's impossible to move the ship."

Sedberry replied, "Okay, then. We'll just have to do the impossible."

During the preparations, Sedberry stayed in contact mostly with Ross, whose home was the navy. Throughout his rough childhood in Kansas, Ross had been shuttled from one foster family to another. He finally found stability in his life when he enlisted in the navy at the age of 18. After graduating first in his class from machinist's mate school in Norfolk, Virginia, Ross eventually was assigned to the *Nevada*'s engineering and propulsion crew, better known as the "black gang." They operated the ship's boilers, turbines, propulsion system, and dynamo rooms. He dealt with what the sailors kiddingly called the ship's junk—the machine shops, metal smiths, hydraulics, generators, and electricity.

In 1940, Ross was promoted to machinist warrant officer and given charge of the ship's forward dynamo room. The forward and aft dynamo rooms contained the controls for the large electrical generators that kept the battleship running, including feeding power to her guns and lighting her corridors belowdecks.

When Ross realized that the fleet was under attack, he instinctively shelved any ideas that he would be celebrating his thirty-first birthday Monday with his fiancée, Helen, a graduate student at the University of Hawaii.

"We're obviously in an emergency situation," he told his 27-man crew. "The *Nevada* is going to need power to get under way." Ross directed them to gear up the turbines for departure and to maintain, at all costs, the generators and air compressors that were giving the *Nevada* power to fire her guns.

Hill, meanwhile, headed up a ten-man line-handling detail to "single up" all the hawsers. It was their job to release most of the mooring lines from the quays but to keep a single line on each quay tethered to the ship until the boilers had worked up enough steam to power the propellers. While dive-bombers and Zeros swarmed over the *Nevada*, Hill and his men hustled down the gangway, jumped into the water, and swam to the quays, totally unprotected, to help free the ship.

Minutes after the attack began, Mass aboard the *Solace* was abruptly concluded. As a lieutenant commander, Ruff needed to return to the *Nevada* ASAP, so he took possession of one of the hospital ship's motor launches. He and the coxswain who was operating the boat kept a wary eye above as the attackers blitzed the harbor. During the harrowing ten-minute trip, the coxswain was forced to zigzag when a Zero strafed the boat, but none of the bullets struck the two men.

As the launch neared the *Nevada*, Ruff spotted three sailors who had been swept off the deck by the *Arizona's* explosion and were floundering in the water. He began pulling them in. As he brought the last of the oil-covered seamen aboard, the boat was strafed again, so the coxswain steered the launch under the *Nevada's* stern for protection. When the threat passed, the launch brought Ruff to the ship's accommodation ladder.

He climbed onto the deck and then went up to the navigation bridge. On the way, he felt the intense heat from the burning *Arizona*. Upon reaching the bridge, Ruff was briefed by Sedberry, who said, "We're close to getting under way. But we don't have a navigator."

"You do now," Ruff replied. He snatched several charts off the shelf, spread them out on a table, and studied them for depths and identifying navigable landmarks.

From belowdecks, Thomas figured he had done all he could in central station, so he climbed the ship's 80-foot access shaft to the bridge and joined the other two. Under Thomas's directions, the ship's damage had been stabilized and the engines and rudder had been tested. Maneuvering a 583-foot-long, 28,000-ton battleship unassisted would be no easy task, especially given that she was severely damaged and partially flooded. And then there was the issue of so little clearance—no more than 30 feet.

Turning to Sedberry, Thomas said, "It's going to be a tight squeeze, and you have to do it without any help."

"What do you mean 'without any help'?" Sedberry replied. "I have you, Ruff, Hill, and Ross, and the gutsiest crew in the navy. I have all the help I need."

Thomas's tension eased. "We've been training for this our whole careers," he said. "We're ready." He pulled out a pen and hastily scrawled in the ship's log: "Urgently necessary to get under way to avoid destruction of ship." When he finished, he told the others in the bridge, "It's now or never."

With Sedberry manning the helm, Ruff navigating, and Thomas conning (giving the orders for the ship's lines, engines, and rudder), the *Nevada* began backing away from her berth.

It was 8:40 A.M., about the time the first wave of Japanese planes began returning to their aircraft carriers. The *Nevada*'s guns, which had already brought down three enemy planes, were still firing at the remaining Zeros, whose relentless pilots chose to make one more pass at the sinking and damaged ships.

One of the Zeros dived on the *Nevada*, shot up her forecastle, and then fired several rounds at the mooring quays. Hill and the others, who had cast off the lines from the quays, leaped into the water. Whether Hill was hit by a bullet or a piece of shrapnel, he didn't flinch, but his arm was bleeding badly.

Seeing the *Nevada* begin to back up, Hill shouted from the water, "You're not leaving without me!" Using strong powerful strokes, he reached the accommodation ladder and, along with the rest of his men, boarded the slowly moving ship.

On the deck, sailors were aiding their wounded shipmates while others battled fires or reloaded their weapons. Everyone wondered if the enemy planes would try to finish them off with another attack. The seamen didn't wait long for the answer. A new wave of Japanese aircraft—many of them high-level bombers—were filling the skies.

In the wheelhouse, Sedberry eased the *Nevada* in reverse until her stern bumped into a dredging pipeline. Then, calling on her starboard engine, Sedberry swung the bow to port and steered clear of the burning *Arizona*. Lining up landmarks on Ford Island, Ruff fed Thomas positions and recommended courses.

The ship moved alarmingly close to the blazing *Arizona*. For the gunners on the starboard side of the *Nevada*, she was too close. The blistering heat from the flames caused first- and second-degree burns on their faces and arms because the men refused to abandon their guns. Along the ammunition line for the starboard antiaircraft batteries, sailors suffered burns because they had to shield the shells from the extreme heat with their bodies so the rounds wouldn't explode.

"Those flames are so close I could light a cigarette from here without a match," Thomas said from the bridge.

Lines were tossed to sailors who had jumped or been blown off the deck of the *Arizona*. The men were brought aboard the *Nevada*, where Hill put them to work helping man the five-inch guns, taking over for those who had been shot, severely burned, or killed.

It was hardly full steam ahead, but there was enough power for the *Nevada* to move at five knots an hour along the battered Battleship Row. With her guns firing, she headed down the south channel of Pearl Harbor toward the entrance to the sea.

Hundreds of fighting men on the badly damaged ships and bombed docks stopped what they were doing to catch a glimpse of her break for freedom. The sight of her tattered American flag flapping in the breeze against a smoke-filled backdrop stirred their souls and boosted their morale. Onlookers cheered and whooped, waving and thrusting their clenched fists triumphantly in the air. To them, she was the ship that couldn't be sunk. Her dramatic defiance electrified seamen and Marines throughout the harbor, inspiring them to rally from this devastating attack. She symbolized that, yes, there was still plenty of fight left in the Americans.

After being shrouded in smoke from the fires, the *Nevada* cleared the end of Battleship Row. Sedberry now faced another tricky move as the ship approached a dredge that was connected by a lengthy pipeline to Ford Island. There was only a narrow opening between the dredge and the eastern shore of the harbor for the *Nevada* to slip through, with no margin for error. Under normal circumstances, it was a difficult passage with help from a harbor pilot and tugboats. Even though he had none assisting him, Sedberry confidently snaked the ship through as if she were no bigger than a family pontoon boat.

But the peril was only mounting. Accompanied by Zeros, enemy fighter bombers in tight formation were dropping their cylinders of death onto the ships again. A bomb penetrated the *Nevada*'s forecastle and blew up belowdecks. The blast caused further weakening of the steel plates on the port side of the hull, which were already leaking heavily from the torpedo.

Then another bomb struck, this one exploding in the ventilation shaft, triggering a flash fire. Ross, who was working in the forward dynamo room below one of the air ducts, took the hot blast of air full in the face. Blinded by the searing heat, he screamed in agony. He couldn't open his eyes because they hurt too much. Overpowering smoke began pouring into the small room. Knowing that the smoke likely carried poisonous fumes that could cause permanent lung damage or even death, he shouted to the crew in the compartment, "Get out! Get out now!"

The men charged out of the room, but when they realized he had stayed behind, they yelled, "You need to leave, too!"

"I'll go soon enough," Ross replied. He knew that if the forward dynamo room failed, the ship would lose power and the ability to fight back. Her antiaircraft guns wouldn't work, pumps would fail, and communication throughout the ship would be lost. "I have to shift the power to the aft dynamo room," he told the crew.

"But that could take at least fifteen minutes, and it's getting harder and harder to breathe," a shipmate said.

"If I don't make the transfer, this ship will be a sitting duck," Ross countered. "I'll stay in touch by phone. I'm all right."

Except he wasn't. He didn't tell the crew that his eyes were scorched and he couldn't see. Incredibly, Ross had prepared for such a possibility. Ever since he arrived on the ship, he had been practicing how to operate the control panel and the switches blindfolded. Now that he was blind—with luck, only temporarily—he felt confident he could tell by touch which switches and controls had to be flipped, turned, or pushed. The only question in his mind was *Can I do it all before I pass out from the fumes?*

Alone in the smoke-filled room, he inhaled through his T-shirt, which he had pulled over his nose, and then held his breath as long as he could. Each time he inhaled, however, his lungs ached and triggered a violent coughing jag that hurt his sides. He wished some of his crewmen were with him to speed up the transfer, but he wasn't willing to call them back and risk their lives. He resolved to continue by himself. *I can't let the ship die!*.

Feeling his way along the control panel, Ross made the necessary adjustments and flipped the required switches that would transfer control of the ship's electrical power to the aft dynamo room, where his men remained in constant contact with him.

Five minutes went by, then ten. They could tell his voice was getting weaker. After about 12 minutes, he whispered in the phone, "God help me." Then the line went silent.

"Ross! Ross! Answer me!" a crewman pleaded over the phone. But there was no response.

Fearing he was either dead or unconscious, the crew rushed into the toxic room, now so thick with smoke they couldn't see him at first, lying on the floor, not breathing. They picked him up and carried him to another compartment, where a corpsman revived him.

Barely able to speak because the fumes had damaged his vocal chords and also left him groggy, Ross had difficulty explaining to the men that he had passed out before he had completed the final tasks. By the time his head had cleared, he learned that the temperature inside the forward dynamo room had soared to over 140 degrees. "I have to go . . . back in there . . . and secure the exhaust . . . in the forward condenser," he said, his sentence interrupted by constant hacking.

"You can't," said a crewman. "It's too dangerous."

"If I don't . . . it could cause . . . an explosion," Ross replied, coughing.

"You nearly died in there," said another sailor.

"I know . . . what I'm doing," Ross snapped. When the crew tried to restrain him, Ross ordered, "Get out . . . of my way!"

Still not aware that he couldn't see, they reluctantly let him go. He lurched down the passageway to the forward dynamo room. Taking a deep breath, he went into the poisonous, super-heated room and stumbled around until he found the cutoff valve and shut it to prevent a deadly blast. When he came out, he collapsed again, this time in the arms of crewmen who carried him topside so he could breathe fresh air. But they stayed behind cover because planes were still attacking the ship.

The Nevada was now the enemy's top target. The Japanese pilots badly wanted to bomb her because they would get a special medal for sinking a battleship. But just as important, sinking her in the middle of the shallow channel would make it extremely difficult for other big ships to get around her and out into the open water. Pilots, who had been lining up their planes to attack other vessels, turned away from their intended targets and converged on the Nevada.

While her guns kept up a steady volley against the enemy, Sedberry changed course several times, trying to make it difficult for the enemy to score any more direct hits. Swarming over her, the bombers took turns assaulting the ship. Two more bombs rattled her, touching off new fires. Near misses sent her heaving and rolling and sprayed her with giant fountains of water. Smoke from her many blazes and her steady gunfire swirled around her, becoming so thick that sometimes she disappeared from view.

One of the near misses struck the destroyer USS *Shaw*, which was undergoing repairs in a floating dry dock, just as the *Nevada* passed her. The explosion ripped off the bow of the *Shaw*, sank the dock, and hurled flaming wreckage onto the *Nevada*'s decks.

Then another bomb landed on the *Nevada*'s starboard side, sending flames roaring up the forecastle and catapulting shrapnel above her masts. The blast wiped out an entire gun crew and killed most of another. Dead and wounded gunners were swiftly replaced by others—even those who were not trained on them—to keep the weapons firing. Teams of two and three men were now doing the work that normally required seven to eight.

Stepping out onto the bridge, Ruff, whose legs were black-and-blue from being banged around by the explosions, looked up and saw several bombs falling toward the ship. He decided those big black things weren't worth watching anymore because there was nothing he could do to stop them. He returned to his charts, deciding he would do his job and let fate decide whether he lived or died. The bombs he had spotted fell in the water within yards of the ship.

As the harassed *Nevada* continued on her stunning run, Ruff wondered, *Is there any chance in the world we can reach the sea?* The ship was under merciless attack, and yet it was still floating, still moving, still fighting.

"Look," said Thomas, pointing to the top of the naval district water tower. Signal flags had been hoisted from headquarters ordering the *Nevada* to "stay clear of channel." The order had come from Vice Admiral William Pye, who feared that the *Nevada* would be sunk in the channel and bottle up the harbor.

Thomas pounded the table in frustration. "We can't disobey orders and continue our run, even though I think we can make it," he told Ruff and Sedberry and the soaking-wet Hill, who had just joined them. "But we can't stay here in the channel, either."

"We have to make a decision fast," Ruff said.

The four agreed they would turn her into the much shallower water off Hospital Point on the east side of the channel and drop anchor there. That way, no matter what happened to her, she wouldn't sink or block the waterway.

"I'll run down to the foredeck and prepare to drop anchor," Hill told Ruff. "If radio communications are lost, just wave your hat as a signal when you want me to do it."

Hill hurried off. Even though the Japanese saw that the *Nevada* was going to beach herself, they didn't let up. In fact, the pilots seemed more intent than ever on trying to destroy her once and for all. They released a cluster of bombs just as Sedberry nosed the ship into the mud near a sugarcane field, ending the shortest, most amazing unscheduled voyage in the annals of naval history.

Out in the open, Hill readied the anchor windlass. Because communication had been broken, he turned around and looked toward the bridge for the signal from Ruff. Hill never saw the three bombs that were hurtling straight down until it was too late. They struck the forecastle in rapid succession, pitching Hill and several others over the bow.

As the second wave of planes headed off to their aircraft carriers, sailors were battling a dozen fires aboard the *Nevada*. The seriously injured Ross, who refrained from telling anyone that his vision was limited to seeing only fuzzy shapes, faked his way into helping shipmates fight the blazes. But his strength was giving out and his breathing was labored.

Then word reached him that smoke was filling the aft dynamo room where his loyal crew was working to maintain the ship's power. "We must rescue them!" he shouted. Following other sailors, Ross felt his way through the passageways until he entered the stricken room, which was thick with noxious fumes and smoke.

Coughing and wheezing, the sight-impaired warrant officer crawled around until he found a crewman who was passed out on the floor. Ross lifted him, draped him over his shoulder, and then staggered out of the room. In terrible pain and with difficulty breathing, Ross made it almost to the top deck before he lost consciousness and fell in a heap with the seaman he had just rescued.

After the ship was beached, Thomas and Ruff left the bridge to focus on damage control. Around 9:15 A.M., Ruff met Captain Scanland, who had finally boarded the ship. Scanland said he left his family in Honolulu once he realized the Japanese were attacking. He battled his way through streets clogged with panicky civilians and chaotic traffic to reach the dock, where he commandeered a launch and then, while avoiding strafing planes, motored through the bloody, oily waters until he caught up to the *Nevada*.

Ruff briefed the captain and then helped direct damage-control parties in trying to put down fires and stem the flooding in lower compartments. Squelching the flames proved difficult because most of the ship's water pipes had been ruptured. Under Thomas's direction, sailors were frantically patching and splicing hoses and pipes. Four tugboats, which carried hoses and pumps, had arrived and began spraying water from the harbor onto the flames. Meanwhile, the wounded and the dead were being taken off the ship and transported to the hospital or the morgue.

Shortly after Ross was revived, a friend of his who was a pharmacist's mate (corpsman) came up to him and said, "I found Mr. Hill on the port side of the ship. He's dead."

Around the same time, the wind and current caught the *Nevada*'s stern and swung her completely around. Fearing that she could slide back and block the channel, Scanland ordered the ship moved to a safer area. With the help of two tugs, she backed up across the channel and beached herself stern first off Waipio Point at 10:45 A.M. Within the next couple of hours, all the fires onboard were under control.

Having suffered a torpedo strike and up to ten bomb hits, the Nevada was no longer seaworthy or battle-worthy. But because of the gallant and courageous efforts of her crew, she was saved from a watery grave to fight another day.

Fifty men were killed and 109 wounded on the Nevada.

The ship was refloated and back in service by 1943. She fought in seven major military engagements during World War II, ranging from Iwo Jima and Okinawa to Western Europe. She was the first Allied warship to fire on the coastline during the invasion of Normandy. After the war, she was deemed too old, so she was used as a target ship at ground zero during the 1946 Bikini Atoll atomic bomb tests. Incredibly, she stayed afloat. Remaining as a target ship, she was finally sunk by naval gunfire and torpedoes during training exercises off the Hawaiian coast in 1948.

Donald Ross regained his eyesight and recovered from his injuries. For his gritty determination to help save the ship, he was presented the Medal of Honor by Admiral Chester W. Nimitz on April 18, 1942, becoming the medal's first World War II recipient. Ross later participated in the invasion at Normandy and earned several combat awards. After 27 years of service in the navy, he retired with the rank of captain and went on to operate a dairy farm near Port Orchard, Washington. Recalling his heroics, he told reporters, "I didn't think about fear. I was frightened, but fear didn't control me. The most important things were my men and the ship. These were more important to me than my own life." He died in 1992 of a heart attack at age 81. His ashes were scattered at sea over the final resting-place of the Nevada. A guided missile destroyer was named in his honor.

For his "skill, leadership, and courage," Edwin Hill was awarded the Medal of Honor (posthumously). Hill, who left behind a wife and three children, was also honored with a destroyer escort named after him. "Hill earned his medal for personal heroism, and he's a true American hero," said former shipmate Joseph Taussig. Hill was buried in Hawaii's Punchbowl Cemetery. Whenever Ross visited Hawaii, he always placed flowers at Hill's grave. "Hill was the most outstanding man on any ship I've ever been on," Ross once said.

Francis Thomas received the Navy Cross for his actions during the attack. After the war, Thomas returned to the steel business and stayed in the naval reserve, retiring as a rear admiral. Before his death in 2005 at the age of 100, he used to joke that he "was the only man in the navy ever to receive a medal for running his ship aground."

For some reason, Robert Sedberry, who was killed in action later in the war, and Lawrence Ruff were not honored with a Navy Cross. In his official after-action report, Captain Francis Scanland praised Sedberry for "his calm and effective handling of the wheel." The captain also lauded Ruff "for his invaluable assistance as acting navigator to Lieutenant Commander Thomas, and assistance in an excellent performance of ship handling." Ruff soon commanded his own ship, the USS Dyson, and earned a Silver Star for his actions during the battle for Okinawa. Ruff, who later served in the Korean and Vietnam Wars, spent 35 years in the navy, retiring as a rear admiral. He then earned a master's degree at UCLA and taught in California. He died in 1978 at the age of 72.

At the conclusion of his after-action report, Captain Scanland wrote, "All members of the crew of the Nevada who were aboard during the attack are deserving of special praise. The courage and spirit of the crew both during and after the attack cannot be over-emphasized."

A memorial stands on the shoreline of what is now called Nevada Point near the spot where the Nevada was last beached after her dramatic run.

THE RUNNING BATTLE

More Heroes of the USS *Nevada*

While sailors of the battleship USS *Nevada* were assembling on the fantail for the morning presentation of the colors, the ship's 23-man band tuned up and the Marine color guard moved into place. Ensign Joseph Taussig, Jr., smiled. As the officer of the deck, the fresh-faced recent Naval Academy graduate was in charge of this time-honored ceremony, so he wanted to make sure everything was perfect on this beautiful Sunday. And to him it was.

No one paid attention to the tiny specks dotting the horizon.

A minute later, those specks grew in size and number—dozens upon dozens—all heading toward Battleship Row. And then, unexpectedly, the far side of Ford Island began shaking from a series of explosions.

But curiosity about the surprising booms was not enough to prevent the band leader, Musician 1st Class Oden McMillan, from delaying for even one second the playing of

"The Star-Spangled Banner." After all, it was 8 A.M., time for the American flag to be hoisted. He tapped his baton to strike up the band.

After the first notes rang out, it became obvious that those once tiny specks were aircraft, so numerous their packed formations were darkening the sky. One plane broke off, descended, and dropped a torpedo that silently glided toward the midsection of the USS *Arizona*, moored directly ahead of the *Nevada*. Seconds later, the blast from the underwater missile rocked the *Arizona*.

The band kept playing. The torpedo bomber veered off and as it zoomed over the *Nevada*, the plane's rear gunner fired away at the assembled sailors, Marines, and musicians who were standing in two neat rows. Miraculously, no one was injured, but the Stars and Stripes, now halfway up the mast, was shredded with bullet holes.

Taussig froze in disbelief. "Japs!"

Despite being a hairsbreadth from death, the band played on. McMillan wouldn't think of stopping in the middle of the national anthem. But then another torpedo bomber flew by and strafed the deck. Splinters whizzed in all directions and bullets struck within inches of the men, causing McMillan to stop long enough to silence the music—but only briefly. He began waving his baton again. Without breaking formation, his dedicated band members picked up where they left off and finished the song. Then everyone sprinted toward their assigned battle stations.

After the second strafing, the ship's bugler began blowing general quarters. But with the harbor now reverberating with explosions, ships' Klaxons, and air-raid sirens from nearby airfields, the bugler's horn couldn't be heard. Taussig grabbed the bugle out of the musician's hand and tossed it aside. Sounding the alarm over the PA system, Taussig shouted, "All hands, general quarters! Air raid! Air raid! This is no drill!"

Even though the *Nevada* was the 21-year-old ensign's first assignment, he instinctively knew what to do, partly because he was a third-generation navy man—the son and grandson of navy admirals. His father, Vice Admiral Joseph Taussig, Sr., led the first American warships to Europe in World War I in 1917, and his grandfather, Rear Admiral Edward Taussig, was a naval hero during the Spanish-American War in 1898.

Fresh out of the US Naval Academy at Annapolis, young Taussig had been on the *Nevada* only a few months. Although he was inexperienced, he had made a decision earlier in the morning that typically only a seasoned officer would have considered. The *Nevada* was powered by six oil-fired turbines, and when in port, it kept one boiler heated even though one wasn't enough to move the vessel. Taussig didn't like being on a ship that couldn't get under way relatively quickly—within 30 minutes—compared to the two and a half hours it normally would take for all the boilers to be working. So he had ordered a second boiler lit just to be on the safe side.

There was another reason why he had given the order. When the ensign was at Annapolis, an instructor, E. J. "Gus"

Fee, predicted that Taussig would never graduate. Taussig's reputation as a young rascal had preceded his arrival at the academy. He was throwing dice and playing cards for money by age 11. As a potty-mouthed teen, he annoyed the cops with his wacky sense of mischief that sometimes landed him at the police station. One time, he was nabbed for putting clothes on a nude statue outside the home of a movie star. Taussig was brought before a judge who gave him a choice: Go to reform school or follow his father's footsteps into the Naval Academy. Taussig wisely chose the latter.

He shaped up at the academy and graduated in an accelerated officers' training program. He was then assigned to the *Nevada*, where Fee, who by this time had transferred from the academy to the ship, was the engineering officer overseeing her boilers. On this Sunday morning, Taussig had ordered the second boiler fired up to remind Fee that the ensign—the cadet who wasn't supposed to graduate—was the officer of the deck.

Whatever Taussig's main motivation was for the order, his decision would soon play a key role in the ship's fate.

Now, as the junior gunnery officer of the starboard anti-aircraft batteries, Taussig scrambled up six ladders to a gun director—an enclosure with equipment to help guide the *Nevada*'s defensive fire. Her .50-caliber machine guns fore and aft had already opened up on the attacking torpedo planes. One of her guns fired at a plane as it closed in on the *Nevada*. The bullets tore into the wing, causing it to buckle and break off. The aircraft rolled over and crashed about 100 yards from the ship.

The sailors who witnessed the downing cheered, but their joy was short-lived when a seaman yelled, "Torpedo off the port bow!"

Seconds later, the torpedo plowed into the *Nevada*. The explosion rattled the ship and blew open a huge 45-foot-by-35-foot hole. As water rushed in, she began listing. But swift action by the damage control crew's counterflooding measures kept her on a fairly even keel.

The port five-inch broadside antiaircraft battery continued shooting at the torpedo bombers. A round struck the torpedo that was still attached to the belly of an attacking plane, blowing up the aircraft in midair. Before crewmen had a chance to gloat, the *Arizona* exploded. Taussig was directing fire on the bombers when a Zero roared by on another strafing run. A bullet penetrated the ensign's gun director, went through his left thigh, and slammed into the instrument panel. He didn't feel any pain at first because his body went into immediate shock. His left leg was shattered and in such an awkward position that his foot was lodged under his armpit. Looking at his severe injury, he thought, *That's a hell of a place for a foot to be.*

Shipmates rushed to his aid. "Let's get you out of here," one of them said to him.

"I will not abandon my post," Taussig declared. "I will not be evacuated." He had been taught at the academy that only under the most extreme situations should an officer leave behind his youngest sailors. Even though he was only 21, the sailors in his gun crew were just 17 and 18 and looked up to him for guidance and inspiration. *There's no way I'm leaving them*, he told himself.

"Just put me on a stretcher," he told them. "I can still do my job from here."

They carried him to a safer area in the sky-control platform above the bridge and laid him down. They tried to put a tourniquet above his thigh to stem the bleeding, but it wouldn't hold because the wound was too high up his leg. Eventually, a corpsman arrived and gave Taussig a shot of morphine to lessen the pain that was now growing sharper by the minute. After wrapping the bloody wound in a compression bandage, the corpsman said, "Your leg is in very bad shape."

"I can't worry about that now," Taussig replied. "We have a war to fight." Applying pressure to the top of his thigh with his hands, the gritty ensign continued to direct the gun batteries from his stretcher.

Ensign Ernest Dunlap, Jr., was in his quarters aboard the *Nevada* relaxing in his civilian clothes—a Hawaiian shirt and Bermuda shorts. Because he had Sunday off, he was going to take the morning launch to shore to meet his wife, Shirley, for a day of surfing off Makapu'u Beach on the southeastern tip of Oahu. She had told him she would be waiting in their 1938 Packard at the dock on the other side of the harbor. *Maybe I'll skip breakfast*, he thought. *Shirley is making a big picnic ham for . . .*

"All hands, general quarters! Air raid! Air raid! This is no drill!"

Hearing the alarm over the loudspeaker, the 26-year-old officer threw off his civilian clothes and donned his uniform. He didn't waste time looking for his socks. He did, however, put on his raincoat—a heavy oil slicker—and buttoned it from above his ankles to his neck. It might have seemed silly, but he figured an extra layer of clothes would offer additional protection.

As Dunlap left his quarters, he heard a loud boom that shook the ship so violently he lost his balance and fell hard on his back, knocking the wind out of him. Rising to his feet, he heard someone yell, "We've been hit by a torpedo!" As an acting gunnery officer, he had a long way to run from belowdecks to get to his battle station high up the superstructure and direct the firing of his crew's big 14-inch guns.

After emerging from the hatch onto the main deck, Dunlap saw a low-flying plane strafing the ship. Bullets were zippering the teak deck with holes, making a dotted line straight toward him. *How weird and crazy is this?* he thought. He leaped out of the way a split second before the plane's guns raked the very spot where he had been standing.

When Dunlap reached his post, he began scanning the horizon for enemy ships because that's what 14-inchers were made for—sea battles. Against diving, darting, speedy Japanese planes, his guns were useless.

Hearing that the handling rooms for some of the gun

mounts on the port side were damaged by the torpedo, he used his phone to organize men into bringing up ammunition by hand to the mounted machine guns. He had to shout over the persistent thunder of explosions, whining of planes, and din of constant shooting.

Dunlap felt the heat from the burning *Arizona* and the unsettling vibrations set off by bombs that had narrowly missed the *Nevada*. Wherever he looked in the harbor, he saw unbelievable damage and death. *I can't just sit here like a bump on a log*, he thought. *I can do more good elsewhere.* Even though leaving one's battle station was a serious offense that could lead to a court-martial, Dunlap didn't care. His only desire was to fight back.

He hurried over to the more mobile five-inch guns, found one whose gunner was slumped over dead, and shoved the body out of the way. Settled in behind the gun, Dunlap spotted a torpedo bomber making a sharp turn. It was flying over the dock where his wife had said she'd meet him. *Oh, dear Lord, what is happening to Shirley? Is she safe?* He shook his head as if to clear those worrisome thoughts. *I need to concentrate.* The plane was now making a beeline for the *Nevada*.

Dunlap looked in the gun sight and, calculating distance and range, aimed his weapon at the oncoming plane and fired in short spurts. About 200 yards from the ship, the aircraft burst into flames and cartwheeled into the harbor waters.

*　　*　　*

Thanks in large part to Taussig's decision earlier in the morning to have two boilers fired up, the *Nevada* was the only battleship to make a run for it. As she sailed down the harbor on her dramatic and inspiring voyage, her guns never let up . . . but neither did the enemy's bombardment.

Ensign Robert Thomas, Jr., who was in charge of a starboard antiaircraft battery, stared at the foreboding formations of enemy bombers and thought, *I'm going to die. But I'm going to fight until they kill me.*

"We'll blow them out of the sky!" one of his captains shouted.

"You're right," said Thomas. "We will."

Looking over his shoulder, he spotted Steward's Mate 2nd Class Herman Bledsoe, a 21-year-old African American who often took care of Thomas's quarters. Even though the battery wasn't Bledsoe's battle station, he was hauling shells to the gun crews. "You can't shoot them down without ammo, Ensign Thomas," Bledsoe said with a grin.

No sooner had the words spilled out of his mouth than a bomb hit near them, instantly killing half of Thomas's crew. The force of the explosion launched the 22-year-old ensign 20 feet through the air and onto the deck. It also propelled a rivet into his right leg and shrapnel into his arms and back and gave him a concussion. He landed right next to Bledsoe, whose right arm and shoulder had been torn off by the blast. "Over here!" Thomas shouted to shipmates with stretchers.

Two seamen arrived and tried to help Thomas, but he shook them off. "Take care of him, not me," he told them. Bleeding badly and feeling woozy, Thomas thought, *We must keep those guns firing.* Wobbling back to his post, he gathered replacements for his lost men and continued shooting at the enemy planes. He kept issuing orders, paying no attention to the blood that was steadily dribbling out of his wounds, until he lost consciousness.

Seeing a need to be filled, Boatswain's Mate 1st Class Paul McMurtry left his battle station and organized relief gun crews for the mounting casualties on the antiaircraft batteries. As soon as one gunner went down, another took his place, so Thomas's guns could keep firing.

Thomas was carried to a compartment crammed with wounded sailors. When he regained consciousness, he thought of the Japanese and muttered, "Okay. You tried to kill me but you couldn't."

Looking around the compartment, he noticed there were no corpsmen and that his moaning shipmates were losing blood. Spotting a seaman with a knife, Thomas called him over and said, "Cut my pant legs and shirt off and then tear them into strips for me. I need them for bandages and a tourniquet." After the sailor did what he was told, Thomas ordered, "Now go around and cut off the uniforms of the others and use them for bandages."

*   *   *

When a bomb struck the boat deck on the starboard side, it ignited several fires and set off a box of ammunition, spraying shrapnel that mowed down several sailors. Yeoman 1st Class James Snyder, who had remained on the navigation bridge throughout much of the attack, was forced by flames to leap to safety onto the bridge below. He saw that another ready box of ammo was smoldering near gunners who were unaware of the deadly threat because they were focused on shooting down the enemy. Knowing he had little time before the gunners would be killed by the exploding ammo, Snyder raced over to the smoking box and removed all the rounds in time to save his shipmates' lives.

Another explosion destroyed the galley and started a fire that swept through the No. 9 casemate, wrecking the antiaircraft gun that had been manned by Marine Corporal Joseph Driskell, 25. The blast, which killed several crewmen, had blown him off his feet and heaved him against another gun. He lurched through the flames and smoke and returned to his post. The surviving men of his crew were shocked at his appearance. Most of his clothes had been burned off, and what was left was still smoldering. His bare legs were bleeding badly from large gashes, and his hair and face were seared.

Corpsmen rushed over with stretchers to collect the wounded. When they insisted on treating Driskell, he waved them off, saying, "I'm all right. Take the other guys and let me be. I've got Japs to shoot down."

He joined a different antiaircraft gun crew that was under-manned. But then a bomb disabled that weapon, too. Although the blast knocked him down, Driskell refused to quit. He tottered over to another gun, replacing a gunner who lay dead.

Down below, Chief Shipfitter George Etcell was handling fires and flooding. Learning that a sailor might be trapped in a smoke-filled, flooded compartment, Etcell waded through waist-deep water that was almost scalding. Finding it as difficult to breathe as it was to see, he slogged in the darkness and steaming water until he came upon an unconscious sailor. By now, Etcell was fighting to keep himself from fainting. His legs felt like they were being boiled, his lungs were shutting down, and his eyes were stinging. Relying on his steel will to survive, Etcell put his fellow sailor over his shoulder and carried him to safety.

Another bomb struck the *Nevada*'s bridge and penetrated the No. 6 casemate, where it exploded and sparked a fire. The blast also severed the pipes that were providing circulating water to the water-cooled machine guns high on the foremast for the crew of veteran Marine Gunnery Sergeant Charles Douglas, 35.

Flames shot up along the forward superstructure, endangering Douglas and his men. Concerned that the gun crew would be burned alive, an officer on the deck shouted up, "Abandon your station!"

But Douglas and his men declined to leave. Coping with unbearable heat from the flames and choking smoke, they steadfastly remained at their posts, firing their guns until the weapons overheated from lack of water and seized up. Only then did the men scamper down through the flames to safety.

Ensign Thomas "Tommy" Taylor, 26, on his first sea duty as an officer in charge of the port antiaircraft battery, showed similar tenacity. An explosion from a bomb had broken both his eardrums, leaving him deaf. A strafing run had sent fragments flying deep into his torso and flames had burned his arms. But nothing stopped him. Despite suffering serious injuries, he continued to direct his crew. Inspired by his courage and spirit, the men kept up a steady volley against the unrelenting enemy.

Taylor finally left his post when he saw flames creeping toward other ammunition boxes. Swiftly organizing a fire-fighting team on the port gun deck, he aimed a steady stream of water on the red-hot boxes to keep the ammo from cooking off. When a Zero flew in for a strafing run, Taylor didn't dash for safety. He crouched down and kept watering the boxes, telling the others, "I have to stay so the ammo won't cook off."

Still clutching his nearly torn-off leg, Ensign Taussig kept directing gunfire from his stretcher on a platform that was now getting blackened on the underside by flames. From his perch six stories high, he stubbornly dismissed the pleas of his fellow shipmates to leave. Even if he wanted to get off, he couldn't. The fire had blocked both ladders to the platform, not that he was capable of using either of them in his condition.

Acting on orders to evacuate Taussig, Pharmacist's Mate 2nd Class Ned Curtis climbed the foremast to the sky-control platform during heavy enemy bombing and strafing.

"What are you doing here?" asked Taussig, still gripping his thigh.

"I'm here to help you get down," Curtis replied.

"Go help someone else," Taussig snarled.

Disregarding the order, Curtis examined the ensign's horrific leg injury and put new pressure bandages on them. But by now, growing flames had trapped both men.

From the deck below, Boatswain's Mate 1st Class Robert "Bob" Norman, who was in charge of the No. 4 gun turret, knew that the stranded ensign and corpsman would burn to death if they couldn't get down. "I'm going up after them," Norman told his shipmates. They didn't question him. Having left his childhood home in Iowa to join the navy at 17, Norman had shown leadership ability even though he was only 21.

With rope slung over his shoulder, he scaled the side of the mast like a rock climber. As he worked his way toward Taussig and Curtis, Norman came too close to the flames. The back of his shirt and pants began to smolder, burning his back and legs. Dangling from the mast with one hand, he slapped at the torched clothes with his other hand. As his blackened clothes fell away, he continued his climb until he reached Taussig and Curtis.

"Ensign Taussig, I'm going to get you out of here," Norman told him.

"Leave me alone!" Taussig barked, his eyes peering skyward for the next enemy plane to attack the ship. Then, facing Norman, he declared, "And that's a direct order!"

"I'm sorry, Ensign Taussig," replied Norman, "but this is one order I'm disobeying."

"You'll be in trouble for this," Taussig warned. "I can't leave my battle station."

"No, Ensign Taussig, *you'll* be in trouble. In fact, if you stay here much longer, you'll be dead."

Norman and Curtis strapped the wounded ensign to the stretcher and tied it with two lines that were secured to the mast. Then they hoisted him over the side of the platform and carefully lowered him to the deck through heavy smoke. When he was let down into the hands of waiting sailors, Taussig was still complaining about leaving his post.

Norman sustained minor burns on his way down, but Curtis suffered severe burns when a sharp gust blew flames directly on him. Crying out in pain, he descended the mast until he couldn't hold on any longer and fell about ten feet to the deck. The corpsman was taken belowdecks where he, Taussig, and other wounded waited out the attack.

After the *Nevada* was beached on Hospital Point, Dunlap joined a crew battling numerous blazes on the ship. He was glad he had on the heavy raincoat because it helped protect his body from the flames. Unfortunately, his exposed ankles were burned and so were his shoes.

While he was fighting a fire, a bomb struck so close to him and his crew that the concussive force shoved them overboard into the water. Stunned by the blast, Dunlap had the presence of mind, while treading water, to take off the raincoat before its weight dragged him under the surface.

Noticing a barely conscious sailor beginning to sink. Dunlap swam over to him and said, "I've got you." Swimming with one arm while holding his shipmate with his free hand, Dunlap towed him to the *Nevada*, which was still under heavy attack.

Back aboard the ship, Dunlap was running toward the forecastle to help rescue a group of sailors trapped under rubble, when another bomb slammed near the bow and exploded. Once again, he was tossed in the air. While airborne, Dunlap felt a large, red-hot piece of shrapnel crash into his face. Then everything went black.

When the attack finally ended, Driskell, who was covered in blood from his gashes, grabbed bandages and helped give first aid to the injured. It never dawned on him to use the bandages on his own wounds. Although barely able to walk, he then joined a firefighting team.

Meanwhile, McMurtry worked tirelessly to help evacuate sailors who were severely wounded, comforting them and urging them to hang on. He wrapped a T-shirt around the head of a shipmate who was hovering near death with a severe head wound. McMurtry then carefully carried him to an ambulance.

Thomas was taken ashore and put in the back of a truck bound for the hospital. A shipmate who was groaning loudly on a stretcher was placed next to him. Thomas looked over and saw that it was Bledsoe, his mess steward. Bledsoe quieted down.

"You didn't have to be up there with me," Thomas said. "You could have stayed down in the mess. But you didn't. You carried shells. You're a hero."

Bledsoe didn't hear him. Bledsoe was dead.

A shipmate who had been blown overboard by the last bomb that struck the *Nevada* found Dunlap spread-eagled and floating facedown in the water. When the sailor turned him over, Dunlap wasn't moving. In fact, it seemed he wasn't breathing.

Dunlap was brought ashore, where a harried corpsman took a quick glance at him and said, "He's dead." Several hours after the attack, Dunlap was placed with hundreds of other bodies at the temporary morgue outside Pearl Harbor Naval Hospital.

His wife, Shirley, who had witnessed the entire attack from the dock opposite the *Nevada*'s original berth, walked in numbed horror among the corpses, searching for her husband and praying that she wouldn't find him among the dead. She looked at faces that were burned or crushed and bodies that were missing limbs. The gruesome scene made her sick to her stomach, but it also gave her hope that her missing husband was alive somewhere because she couldn't find him.

After Shirley left, a member of the morgue detail began checking each corpse for anything that would help identify the victim. Suddenly, he heard a slight cough. Combing among the dead, he spotted a battered body that was twitching. "He's alive!" the morgue attendant shouted. "Bring me a stretcher!"

While the attendant waited, he checked the ID in the victim's pocket. It said, "Boatswain's Mate 1/c Ernest H. Dunlap, Jr."

Rushed into the emergency room, Dunlap tried to open his eyes but couldn't. His whole head felt like it had been beaten in with a sledgehammer. He didn't know pain could be this excruciating. Just before he lost consciousness again, he heard a doctor whisper to a nurse, "I doubt if he'll make it through the night."

But Dunlap did make it. And the next day and the one after that, too. When the sailor became fully conscious, the doctor told him, "You have a tough road ahead of you."

The first time Shirley saw Dunlap in the hospital, she cried for joy that he was alive. And she cried for sorrow that he was in serious condition. Shirley could see what he couldn't: The entire right side of his face was smashed, every facial bone shattered. Much of the skin on his face and scalp was burned off. Nothing about him resembled the handsome man she had married six months earlier.

Dunlap reached out and clasped Shirley's hand. Speaking from the left side of his mouth, he murmured, "We're going to be all right. You're alive and I'm alive. We came out of this okay.

I have my arms, my legs, and my head. Yeah, we're going to be all right."

Joseph Taussig, Jr., was awarded the Navy Cross for his bravery. Remaining in the navy, he spent 4 years in and out of military hospitals and underwent 15 operations, but doctors still couldn't save his leg. It was amputated in 1946. Three days later, he returned to active duty and rose to the rank of captain. After the war, Taussig earned a law degree and taught at the Naval Academy. Throughout the 1960s and '70s, he worked for various government agencies before becoming the navy's assistant undersecretary for safety. He died in 1999 at the age of 79 and is buried at the United States Naval Academy Cemetery.

In the years before his death, Taussig was bothered that Bob Norman never received a medal for helping save his life. Without Norman's knowledge, Taussig lobbied the Pentagon into giving what he termed "the unsung hero" the recognition he deserved. Taussig's efforts paid off. In 1998—57 years after the Pearl Harbor attack— Norman was presented with the military's third-highest combat award, the Silver Star, in a ceremony at the Naval Academy.

Norman, who rose to the rank of captain, said the medal was "worth more than all the money in the world." He told reporters at the time, "It's coming way late in the game, of course. But it's an honor. I'm proud to receive it. I spent thirty-six and a half years in the navy, through World War II, Korea, and Vietnam, and I'm proud of all of it." Norman, who worked for an international engineering firm after leaving the navy, died in 2013 at the age of 93.

Ensigns Harold Christopher and Frederick Davis were honored with the Navy Cross posthumously after they were killed while taking charge of antiaircraft batteries that were undermanned. The medal also was awarded to Seaman 2nd Class Louis Gombasy, who, although wounded, helped clear mooring lines, assisted injured shipmates, and fought fires. Ensign Allen Huttenberg, who maintained effective fire on an undermanned battery even though he was seriously wounded, also received the Navy Cross.

Ernest Dunlap, Tommy Taylor, Joseph Driskell, and Robert Thomas recovered from their wounds and were awarded the Navy Cross for their courageous actions during the attack. They all returned to the war.

Dunlap made the navy his career and retired as a rear admiral. He died in 1968 at the age of 53.

Taylor also was a career navy man, taking command of several ships. Leaving the navy in 1963, he set up his own law practice in Virginia. He died in 1983 at the age of 68.

Driskell, who also earned a Bronze Star and a field promotion to second lieutenant for his fighting in the Battle of Iwo Jima, retired from the Marine Corps in 1953. He died in 1997 at the age of 81.

Thomas served in the navy until he retired in 1964. He became an official for Orange County, California, and was its chief administrative officer from 1968 to 1986. He died in 2015 at the age of 95. He often said that he never got over Herman Bledsoe's death. "Although he was black, our blood was the same color," said Thomas, referring to the era when the navy discriminated against African Americans. "He came topside to help carry ammo and was killed in action. So he won no honors, no distinctions, just a 21-year-old doing his job. I've always considered him a hero."

Charles Douglas, Paul McMurtry, George Etcell, James Snyder, and Ned Curtis also received the Navy Cross for their brave actions on December 7, 1941. Writing a letter to his wife, Catherine, from his hospital bed in Pearl Harbor four months later, Curtis said, "I'll carry a scar as well as the Cross as a memento of the attack."

"NO ONE ATTACKS AMERICA AND GETS AWAY WITH IT!"

The Hero of Kaneohe Naval Air Station

Bleeding from bullet holes and shrapnel wounds, Chief Petty Officer John Finn stood defiantly behind his overheated machine gun. Even though he was totally exposed out in the open and losing strength, he continued to fire at the screaming Japanese planes that were destroying his small naval air station 12 miles east of Pearl Harbor.

His only cover was from the curling smoke from a nearby hangar that was burning out of control. Finn had no fear, only rage. *I'm gonna shoot 'em down 'til they shoot me dead*, he vowed to himself.

Armed with several lengthy belts of ammunition, he maintained a furious pace throughout the first of three attacks on the base. The loud *rat-a-tat-tat* fire from his machine gun drowned out the whining of the swooping, diving planes. Finn never thought about his own safety—not even when bullets pierced his body. *They have to pay a price for this! They have to know that they can't get away with a surprise attack without losing their own lives!*

Every time he saw the red "meatball" under the wings of the planes, he seethed and used it as a bull's-eye. When he ran through one ammo belt, he swiftly loaded another into his weapon.

Finn was so focused on fighting back that he had no idea how badly hurt he was. He wasn't aware that the loss of blood was sapping his mental sharpness and his energy. The only things keeping him going were the adrenaline and the fury flowing through his veins.

Finn was now a target that the enemy needed to silence for good. While he was fixated on trying to down a dive-bomber roaring low toward the base, he failed to notice that another plane was zooming in on his right and taking deadly aim at him.

Less than two hours earlier, Finn had been lounging with his wife, Alice, in their palm tree–shaded bungalow. Their house was a mile away from the Kaneohe Naval Air Station, where the 32-year-old chief petty officer headed a 35-man unit in charge of ammunition for one of the base's three squadrons. He loved the navy and was proud that even though he was a seventh-grade dropout, he had made something of himself after enlisting at the age of 17.

The air station, located on Kaneohe Bay, was home to 36 twin-engine seaplanes known as PBYs, which were anchored in the water, tied down on a concrete parking ramp, or sheltered in one of three hangars. The flight crews had been flying routine patrols searching for Japanese submarines that might try to sneak into nearby Pearl Harbor.

On this lazy Sunday morning, about 7:50 A.M., Finn and Alice were good-naturedly trying to convince the other to get out of bed and make the coffee. They stopped their banter after hearing planes and machine gun fire. "That's odd," Finn told Alice. "It sounds like a lot of single-engine planes, but our PBYs have two engines. Whoever they are, they're not following the usual flight pattern. And who is firing machine guns? If anyone is supposed to be firing one, I'd know about it."

As he hopped out of bed, he heard someone knocking on the front door. Louise Sullivan, the wife of one of his men, Eddie "Sully" Sullivan, who lived next door, stood on the stoop, looking pale and scared. "Some sailors drove by and yelled that they want you down at the hangar right away," she said in a quavering voice. Then she turned and ran off.

Perplexed, Finn jumped into his 1938 Ford. Before Finn pulled away, Sullivan hopped into the front seat. On the short drive to the base, they heard a frightening roar coming from behind them. Finn looked at his side-view mirror and was startled to see a single-engine plane zooming toward them just a few feet off the ground. When the plane came abreast of the car, it banked toward the air station, revealing the red symbol on the underside of the wing. "Sully!" Finn gasped. "This is the real McCoy. It's the Japs!"

He stomped on the gas pedal, and when they reached the

top of a hill that overlooked the bayside base, they were staggered by the chaos playing out in front of them. Planes were dive-bombing the airfield, triggering eruptions of orange balls of fire. Enemy machine guns were raking the parked PBYs with incendiary bullets as panic-stricken sailors were running helter-skelter in confusion and fear. The vicious strafing mowed down men who failed to duck behind cover in time. Smoke was swelling up from scores of fires. "My God, all hell is breaking loose!" Finn exclaimed.

He floored the gas pedal and drove straight into the mayhem. After the car screeched to a stop, he and Sullivan jumped out and sprinted 150 yards toward the armory. On their way, a plane skimming only 30 feet off the ground fired several rounds that kicked up dirt right next to them.

Inside, they found men crouched under their desks. "The war is on!" Finn bellowed. "The Japs are here!"

One of the sailors muttered, "I didn't know they were *that* sore at us."

"Come on!" Finn yelled. "We've got to fight back!"

"With what?" countered another sailor. "We don't have any antiaircraft guns."

"We'll fight 'em with whatever we've got." Finn doled out the few machine guns and ammunition that had been stored inside. Some of the weapons were from World War I, but he had no choice. "Rifles, pistols, whatever you can find," he said. "Start shooting!"

Each PBY carried four mounted weapons, two .50-caliber and two .30-caliber machine guns. But every one of the planes was either burning or damaged. On his orders, sailors raced toward the smoking wreckage and removed guns and ammunition before the gas tanks of several planes exploded. Many burning planes were just too dangerous to get near.

Making a mad dash to his squadron's hangar, Finn pointed to the ten 500-pound, TNT-loaded depth charges that were kept inside for use by the PBYs against enemy submarines. "Sully, get them out of here," he told Sullivan. "If those strafing Japs hit one of the depth charges, the hangar will blow up." The hangar next door was already in flames.

"Where should I take them, Chief?" Sullivan asked.

"Put them in the bushes [several hundred yards away] and scatter them with plenty of distance between them."

Right outside the armory door, two of his men were firing machine guns at the planes. "Move away from the armory so you can see the Japs better," he told young Radioman 2nd Class Robert "RJ" Peterson.

Looking out over the bay, Finn spotted a Japanese plane approaching them low and firing its machine guns. After dodging the bullets, Finn snatched the .30-caliber machine gun from Peterson's hands. "I have more experience," the 15-year navy veteran told him. Finn carried the weapon out about 20 yards from the building into the middle of an open concrete parking area so he could see in all directions. The sheer number of enemy planes covering the otherwise beautiful morning sky left him more angered than awed. Most of the planes were heading west, which meant only one thing: *They're going to bomb Pearl Harbor!*

Filled with a rage he had never felt before, Finn raised the machine gun, which weighed more than 30 pounds, and began firing it in the sky. "I want to give the Japs a warm welcome!" he shouted. But without having a tripod to rest the heavy weapon on, the strong, five-foot nine-inch Finn found it almost impossible to shoot with any accuracy.

He dragged one of the base's two instruction stands to a completely exposed section of the airplane parking ramp and secured the gun to a tripod. Turning to Peterson, he said, "I know it's out in the open with no cover, but just keep shooting this weapon."

Finn then commandeered a heavier .50-caliber machine gun and set it up on a tripod made out of spare pipes. The tripod, which sat on a wooden platform, had been built for training purposes only and wasn't designed for real combat. But this was the hand Finn was dealt, and he was going to play it. He lugged the 80-pound weapon and tripod out from the hangar to a spot on the parking area where he was fully exposed again, and yelled to his fellow sailors, "No one attacks America and gets away with it!"

When 5 bombers flew overhead at about 4,000 feet, Finn fired an entire hundred-round ammo belt at them, but to no avail. Then he saw tiny black objects coming out of the planes and falling toward the base. It took a moment before his brain recognized them. To the sailors closest to him, he shouted, "Get out of here! Those bombs have our address!"

He ran into the armory, ducked under a stairwell, and

threw his arms over his head. After three thunderous, earth-rocking booms, he hurried outside to assess the damage. One of the bombs had made nearly a direct hit on the gun he was firing, leaving a crater 12 feet in diameter in the busted-up concrete. The rubble had buried most of his ammo. *If I hadn't seen those bombs in time, I'd have been blown into jelly,* he thought. *I'm lucky I can run fast.*

He went back to firing his weapon. Every passing minute, Finn was getting increasingly irate, not only at the enemy but also at himself for his failure to shoot one out of the sky. *My God,* he told himself, *can't you bring down even one of those planes?*

Some of them were diving so close to him that he could see the pilots' faces—and they were laughing. That made him even more furious.

Taking his eyes off the enemy briefly, he noticed that the depth charges were still in the hangar. "Where's Eddie Sullivan?" he shouted to a group of sailors.

"We don't know, Chief," came the reply. "He was here a little while ago."

Did he run and hide? Finn wondered. *I can't believe he'd be a coward, but who knows what people will do in combat.*

During a break in the action, Finn helped carry the wounded to a safer area. "We need more weapons!" he shouted.

The only remaining machine guns were in the burning planes. Peterson left the .30-caliber weapon he had been firing and picked up a fire extinguisher. Then he ran toward a parked plane that was smoking. "I think I can save it," he shouted.

As he sprayed the smoldering fire in the PBY, flames from the plane next to it set off deadly rounds of ammunition. Peterson ducked and kept spraying until the fire was completely out on the PBY. Although the plane was blackened inside, the cockpit wasn't damaged. The PBY would be flyable.

But bullets were still cooking off from the other burning plane. Rather than dash for safety, Peterson uncoupled a .30-caliber machine gun from the PBY he had saved and carried it away. Seconds later, flames reached the gas tank of the other plane, igniting an explosion that caused Peterson to stumble. Unscathed, he stood up and handed off the weapon to a crewman to use.

Within a few minutes, nine enemy planes came in for another attack. Finn, Peterson, and their comrades fired their weapons at every one of them. The more Finn shot, the more he caught the pilots' attention. Soon every strafing run included gunfire directed at the tough-as-nails navy man. But he just kept on shooting. Even when he got grazed by a bullet and then struck by shrapnel, he never wavered.

But when bullets ripped into the platform, sharp bits of wood and metal pierced his legs and chest. Finn stopped shooting and dropped to his knees in pain. Seeing blood seeping through his pants, he gazed skyward and hollered, "Now you've really ticked me off!" He took a few deep breaths, got back on his feet, and continued firing at the enemy.

Then another plane descended on the base. Finn was so focused on stopping the strafing run that he didn't realize a second dive-bomber was flying low directly at him. It began peppering the parking area where he was shooting. Once again, Finn was struck, this time in the upper left arm and right thumb. "Ahh!" He let go of the trigger and studied his latest wounds. One of the bullets had gone through a fleshy part of his bicep, and although it hurt, he told himself, *It's no big deal.* His injured arm, though, was losing all its strength and becoming useless.

Finn kept shooting until the barrel of his machine gun glowed red-hot. Low on ammo, he stepped off the platform and limped into the smoke-filled armory, where he draped more heavy belts of ammo over his shoulders.

On his way back to the platform, he spotted Sullivan on a tractor, pulling the depth charges out of the hangar. With total disregard for his own safety, Sullivan had been removing the explosives just as he had been ordered to do and hiding them in the brush even during repeated strafing runs. *Good ol' Sully,* Finn thought. *I never should have doubted him.*

Hobbling past a group of sailors who were firing pistols and rifles from behind a truck, Finn yelled, "We'll never give up!"

One of them then said, "Hey, Finn, you're not going back out there, are you?"

"Yep. That's my post."

Just then a bullet slammed into his thigh, and he tumbled to the ground. The men charged out toward him, but he gestured to go back. "It's nothing," he grunted. "The bullet went straight through. It's only a flesh wound."

He gathered his ammo belts and stumbled back onto the platform, where he loaded his weapon and began shooting again with his one good arm while standing on his one good leg. Just when he had an enemy plane in his sights, the gun jammed. *Can my luck get any worse?* As he feverishly worked to unjam the weapon, a bomb exploded a few yards away, flinging small pieces of shrapnel deep into his belly. He fell backward from the impact, leaving him woozy.

His once crisp white shirt and pants were now soaked with blood. After giving himself a quick assessment of his injuries, he told himself, *I'm hurt, but it's not that serious. Time to get back on my feet.*

Finn pulled himself up and worked on the machine gun until it was operating again. He had no idea how many planes, if any, he had hit, damaged, or destroyed. All he knew was that he would never quit shooting.

During another brief lull, he felt the pain from his wounds growing in intensity. One of the sailors came over to him and said, "Finn, you're a bloody mess. I'll get you a corpsman."

"Don't worry about me," Finn replied with a wince. "It looks worse than it is. Just keep manning your guns. Now get back to your post!"

Moments later, Finn spotted a Japanese plane in the distance heading directly toward him. *Here's my chance,* he thought. The plane dropped lower and kept on its straight-ahead course parallel to the ground before flying into a black cloud of smoke at the far end of the air station. *Wait, wait, don't shoot too soon. When he comes out of that smoke, then I'm gonna let him have it.*

As the plane emerged from the thick haze, everything turned into slow motion for Finn. He saw its propeller turn the smoke in a wispy circle, reminding him of the holiday wreath that Alice had hung on the front door the day before. Now only ten feet above the ground, the plane looked like it was going to fly straight into Finn's gun barrel. Then he saw bursts of light flashing from its wings, its deadly machine gun bullets striking the ground in a pattern that was tracking right toward him.

Finn's sweaty, bleeding fingers gripped the trigger. The plane was so close now that he could see the pilot's face. *He's grinning at me! Well, not for long!*

Finn squeezed the trigger and ripped off several rounds at the propeller before the plane shrieked by only a few feet over his head. Finn swiveled his machine gun around and fired at the tail. Suddenly, the plane started spewing smoke. The engine coughed, sputtered, and burst into flames. The plane banked sharply to the left and plunged into the woods.

"I got him!" Finn yelled. "I got him!"

He jumped up in exultation and promptly collapsed on the platform in agony. One of the enemy's bullets had struck Finn's foot and torn away his shoe. The pain was too intense to ignore.

"Finn," yelled a corpsman who was tending to a wounded sailor about 50 yards away. "Let me help you!"

"Stay where you are," Finn ordered. "You take care of the others first. I've been scratched up, that's all." He was more than scratched. Finn had bullet holes in his arm and thigh and shrapnel wounds in his legs, stomach, and chest. He was losing blood. But he wasn't ready to give up; he wasn't willing to abandon his post. So what if he was badly wounded. It was important to him to keep fighting back. *No matter what,* he told himself, *those Japs can't go unpunished—not by me, my comrades, or my country.*

More than once, fellow sailors begged him to leave his post and seek medical help, but he waved them off. "I'm not ready yet," he yelled at them.

Finally, after nearly two hours of fighting, the raiders left for good, having dropped 18 bombs on the base. When the last enemy plane had flown off, the air station fell into an eerie silence except for the crackling of the fires. Finn scanned the skies, wondering if more attackers were on their way. But when he looked around, he figured the Japanese had accomplished their mission. They had destroyed virtually the entire air station.

Where hangars once stood, only twisted, charred ruins remained. Every PBY lay bullet-ridden and crumpled, unable to fly. Flames licked out of the broken windows of barracks and other buildings. Men quietly extinguished fires while others carted the wounded and dead off the airfield, which was strewn with wreckage, debris, and litter.

Tears welled up in Finn's eyes. He wished he had done more. He wished he and his men had shot down every plane. He wished the base had bigger and better weapons to defend itself.

As blood oozed out of his arms, legs, feet, hands, chest, and forehead, Finn stumbled off the platform, weakened and in terrible pain. *I need to keep my head clear,* he thought. *I must start organizing a defense in case the Japs return to try to kill the rest of us.*

"Finn," said a superior officer. "You need help. You're in bad shape."

"So is our air station, sir," Finn replied. "I'll see the corpsmen later. But first we've got a lot of work to do here to prepare for the next possible attack. We should bring some semblance of order back to Kaneohe Bay." He knew that his men needed his experience and leadership now more than ever.

Shuffling on one leg, Finn moved slowly because it hurt too much to move at all. With every step, he cringed from the jabbing pain of his shot-up foot. With every breath, he flinched from the stinging pains in his lacerated chest.

"I order you to sick bay," the officer told him. "Now!"

Reluctantly, Finn went to a corpsman, but refused to lie down on a cot. "Just patch me up, and I'll come back later for further treatment," Finn said.

"You really need to be hospitalized," the corpsman insisted.

Finn glared at him. "There's much I have to do. And there's more you need to do for sailors who are in worse shape than me. Put some bandages on me to stop the bleeding and let me out of here."

After the corpsman did what he was told, Finn left to direct men in repairing defenses and setting up machine gun pits around the air station. Most of these weapons were designed for use on the PBYs, so he figured out new ways to mount them in the pits. It was tedious work that went long into the night. Time and again, fellow sailors urged the bloodied petty officer to seek treatment for his wounds, but Finn brushed them off. "Not until the work is done," he said.

Eventually, the superior officer approached him and said, "You have gone above and beyond the call of duty. Now it's time to take care of yourself. Get to sick bay."

"But, sir . . ."

"No 'buts,' Finn. That's an order."

When he limped into the infirmary, Finn looked at the clock and was surprised at the time. It was 2 A.M. Monday morning. He had been going nonstop for more than 18 hours. Despite the late hour, sick bay was still bustling as corpsmen scurried around, tending to dozens of seriously wounded men. *No sense waiting around here for a doctor. I need to go home and check on Alice.*

He shuffled outside and looked for his car. *What are the chances that it isn't damaged? Probably slim to none.* When he reached the back of a bombed-out building, he smiled for the first time since the attack. There was his Ford without a scratch, except the one that Alice had made when she accidentally backed into a jeep a few weeks earlier.

Fatigue had set in and the pain had grown worse by the time he drove home, which, to his relief, wasn't damaged. When he wobbled through the front door, Alice shrieked with a mixture of relief and shock. Thankful he was alive, she tore off his bloody clothes and tended to the shrapnel cuts and bullet holes on his battered body.

"Oh, dear Lord," she said. "I've counted twenty-one wounds on you."

"I'm more shot up than I thought," he said. "I guess it wasn't my day to die."

"I need to get you to the doctor's immediately."

"Later in the morning," he mumbled. "I'm too tired and too hurt to move."

Finn was hospitalized for nearly three weeks while being treated for a broken left foot, bullet wounds in his thigh and arms, deep shrapnel-caused gouges to his chest, stomach, right elbow, and thumb, and a severe gash on his scalp. During his stay, he received terrible news: twenty people, all but two of them sailors and friends of his, were killed in the attack at Kaneohe. They were later buried at the air station.

Finn returned home on Christmas Eve—a bittersweet holiday for the couple. They were incredibly grateful he survived, but in a somber understatement, he told Alice, "The world will never be the same."

Nine months after the surprise attack, Finn, who had been promoted to lieutenant, received the Medal of Honor during a ceremony on the aircraft carrier USS Enterprise, which was docked at Pearl Harbor. With the crew and Alice watching, Admiral Chester W. Nimitz presented Finn with the medal, saying, "Congratulations,

Lieutenant. You have made America proud." Finn blushed and said, "Thank you, sir. I'm just a good old navy man who was doing his job."

Finn served on three ships during World War II. He retired from the navy in 1947, opened a salvage yard, and later, with his wife, Alice, lived on their 93-acre cattle ranch in Pine Valley, California, near San Diego. Over the years, buildings at naval installations were named after him, and in 2015, the destroyer USS John Finn was launched. Finn died in 2010 at the age of 100. He was the last surviving Medal of Honor recipient of the Pearl Harbor attack.

Robert Peterson earned the Navy Cross for manning the .30-caliber machine gun in an exposed position under heavy strafing fire. According to the citation, he "returned the enemy fire with telling effect during three enemy strafing and bomb attacks, with complete disregard for his own safety." The citation added, "Immediately following one attack, he entered a group of blazing planes in which ammunition and gasoline exploded violently. Without assistance he extinguished a serious fire in one plane, saving it from destruction."

CARRYING A HEAVY LOAD

Heroes of the USS West Virginia

In an era of racial discrimination in the navy, the two friends on the USS *West Virginia* made an odd pair. One was a dark-skinned, muscular, six-foot-three, 235-pound seaman. The other was a lily-white, lanky 180-pound baby-faced teenager. Everyone knew the black sailor because he was the ship's heavyweight boxing champion. Few knew the white kid, who had been aboard for only four months.

But 22-year-old Mess Attendant 2nd Class Doris Miller and 17-year-old Quartermaster Striker Arles Cole had plenty in common. Both hailed from Southwestern states, Miller from near Waco, Texas, and Cole from eastern Oklahoma. Both lived hardscrabble childhoods working on family farms that barely provided enough to eat. And both left high school to join the navy.

They shared something else, too: In terms of rank, they were at the bottom of the totem pole. As a quartermaster striker, Cole was a grunt getting on-the-job training in the care of the ship's clocks, navigational instruments, and charts and was drawing the worst shifts as a lookout.

Miller's job was the lowest of the low. At the time, less than 3 percent of sailors in the United States Navy were African American, and all held the lousiest ranks as stewards or cook's assistants. They were called mess boys, seagoing bellhops, or chambermaids of the Braid. (*Braid* is slang for high-ranking officers.) As a mess hall attendant and steward, Miller peeled potatoes, shined shoes, mopped decks, made beds, washed dishes, and served as a waiter for the officers of the *West Virginia*. He was not trained in the ship's weaponry. In fact, because of the color of his skin, Miller was, by unspoken naval tradition, forbidden to even touch the machine guns on deck.

But on the morning of December 7, the unlikely pair became heroes in their own special ways, displaying the same bravery, valor, and spirit as the captain, officers, and crewmen of the *West Virginia*.

After days of training exercises off the Hawaiian coast, most of the warships of the Pacific Fleet had returned to Pearl Harbor by Saturday, December 6. The *West Virginia*—called affectionately "the Wee-Vee" by the crew—anchored beside and outboard of the battleship USS *Tennessee*.

Many of the officers and enlisted men were granted what they termed Cinderella liberty—shore leave that required them to return to the ship by midnight. With what little money they had, Miller and Cole took advantage of this time to buy modest Christmas presents in Honolulu for their respective families.

Miller—whose name Doris was in honor of an aunt—was looking for a special gift for his parents, Connery and Henrietta, who had lovingly raised him and his three brothers on the family farm outside Speegleville, Texas. Toiling in the fields made Miller strong, and he eventually starred in football in high school. But against his parents' wishes, he dropped out after one year and worked as a short-order cook in a diner to help supplement the family's meager income. In 1939, at the age of 19, Miller joined the navy and ended up on the *West Virginia*, where, despite his status as a lowly mess steward, the crew respected him and his boxing skills.

On his Honolulu shopping trip, Cole was hoping to find something that would appeal to his patriotic family, who always sang the praises of America. His father, Albert, a subsistence farmer, had fought in World War I and imparted in his children a sense of duty to serve one's country. After Cole's older brother joined the army, Cole left school in 1940 at age 17 and hitchhiked 90 miles to a recruiting station in Tulsa to enlist in the navy.

Completing his basic training, Cole reported for duty aboard the *West Virginia* in August of 1941. He was learning the ropes from the quartermaster, an enlisted man in charge of, among other things, navigation and the maintenance, correction, and preparation of nautical charts. That meant Cole spent much of his time in the ship's pilothouse and bridge, located in the superstructure high above the main deck.

It was there that he met Miller, who oftentimes served as the steward for Captain Mervyn Bennion. The two enlisted men became friends.

After returning to the ship on that Saturday night, Miller and Cole stowed the Christmas gifts they had bought for their families. Cole had permission to sleep in the pilothouse, where it was cooler than the stuffy crew quarters below, and made himself a little bed on the chart table. Miller headed down to his berth, knowing he would have to get up early to serve breakfast in the junior officers' mess.

Sunday morning, Bennion was shaving in his ship's cabin, recalling in his mind the splendid Saturday evening he had enjoyed dining with friends in Honolulu. Planning to meet them at church within the hour, the 53-year-old skipper finished getting dressed in his white uniform, when a sailor on watch on the bridge rushed in and announced, "Captain, the Japanese are attacking by air!"

Bennion gave the command for the crew to man their battle stations and then hustled to the conning tower on the flag bridge, where he issued orders in a cool but rapid-fire sequence. Gunners were springing into action and the handlers were bringing up ammunition from the holds while the rest of the crew was carrying out their assigned roles.

In less than a minute, Japanese torpedo planes released their torpedoes. Three of them struck the *West Virginia* one after the other, tearing two large holes in her port side and destroying the steering gear and rudder. Then three more torpedoes slammed into her.

Seconds later, enemy bombers flew overhead and dropped two armor-piercing bombs. The first one penetrated the superstructure deck, wrecking the port casemates and causing the deck to collapse into the galley deck below. Four casemates and the galley burst into flames, detonating stowed ammunition.

The second bomb hit farther aft, destroying one of No. 3 turret's two guns. It also wrecked a Kingfisher—a single-engine observation seaplane—that was attached to a catapult. The impact caused a second Kingfisher to fall upside down onto the main deck, rupturing its fuel tanks. The spilled gasoline ignited, burning crewmen in the turret and damaging the turret's other gun.

Then the USS *Arizona*, directly aft of the ship, blew up, spewing flaming globs of oil onto the *West Virginia*'s decks and causing even more fires on her. At the same time, torrents of water were pouring into her port compartments from the massive holes blown open by the torpedoes.

Lieutenant Commander Thomas Beattie, the ship's navigator, reported to Bennion that communications in the conning tower had been knocked out. Referring to the use of runners to pass information back and forth, Beattie said, "Captain, should we establish messenger communication?"

"Yes, by all means," Bennion replied. "It's vital if we're to save the ship."

The torpedo, bomb, and strafing attacks were constantly

shaking the *West Virginia* from bow to stern. Trying to see the damage for themselves, Bennion and Beattie stepped out onto the flag bridge just as a high-level bomb struck the turret of the *Tennessee*, less than a hundred feet away, and exploded. Hot shrapnel from the blast flew in all directions.

Bennion doubled up with a loud, anguished groan and uttered, "I've been hit." He collapsed to the bridge floor. A metal shard had sliced deeply into his abdomen, exposing his intestines. The fragment dug into his left hip and lodged by his spine, causing him to lose all feeling and use of his legs. Collapsing to the bridge floor, he rolled over on his back, grimacing in pain.

In the pilothouse, Cole dropped his coffee mug and charged toward his battle station in central station, deep in the bowels of the ship. To save time, he straddled the handrails of ladders and rode them down for four decks.

On his way, the *West Virginia* shuddered mightily from back-to-back-to-back torpedoes and immediately began to list to port. Cole passed sailors who were bleeding or were burned and others who were wailing in pain or panic. Smoke from burning fuel oil and explosions made it difficult for him to see or breathe.

Fighting hard to keep from losing his nerve, Cole forced himself to keep hustling down another four decks toward his battle station. He reminded himself that on a warship, every man needed to carry out his duty if they were to survive. The

West Virginia shook again from more explosions—he couldn't tell if they were from bombs or torpedoes—that swept him off his feet and slammed him against bulkheads and other sailors.

By the time he reached the third deck, the ship was listing hard to port. Streams of water—some crystal clear and others dark and oily—were gushing through busted steel plates. Because the ship was continuing to tilt dangerously, he had to press his hands against the bulkheads while working his way unsteadily along the center passageway.

As he neared central station, the lights belowdecks dimmed, flickered, and then went out because the generators had flooded. Terror-stricken in the blackness, Cole knew it was useless to go any farther. Cold, oily salt water was quickly rising from his ankles to his knees and then to his waist. He needed to save himself. But which way to go? *Starboard. I need to get to the starboard side.*

Moving away from the flooding in the dark was frustrating and frightening. Every escape route was blocked. Whenever he reached a watertight door, he discovered it had been dogged. He was stuck in a maze that had no exit. *Oh my God,* he thought, *I'm trapped—trapped in a watery tomb.*

Miller was sorting officers' laundry when general quarters was sounded. He immediately headed for his battle station, which was in the antiaircraft battery magazine amidships. Because of his physical strength and size, he had been assigned to go there as an ammunition handler.

Arriving at his post, he saw that it had been destroyed by a torpedo. Then he felt the ship listing to port. Before Miller had a chance to think, a chief petty officer shouted, "We need help carrying wounded men to the battle dressing station!"

Miller didn't need to be told twice. He picked up the nearest wounded sailor and lugged him up to the main deck, where corpsmen were treating the injured. Relying on his size and strength, he ran across the deck to retrieve injured shipmates and carried them to safety on the quarterdeck. Then he went below, and using a mess bench for a stretcher, he helped bring out a sailor with a serious back injury.

With the acrid smell of smoke stinging his nostrils, Miller went back down again, when another explosion jarred the listing ship, plunging the interior into darkness. Lurching from one side to the other on the slippery, slanting floor, he felt his way toward a voice calling out for help. But then a blast rocked the ship and sent Miller crashing against a bulkhead near a berthing compartment. He struck his head hard against a metal pipe and blacked out.

When Beattie, the ship's navigator, saw that Bennion was seriously wounded, he loosened the captain's collar and ordered a sailor on the bridge, "Find a pharmacist's mate and get him back here on the double."

After telling two sailors to stay with the captain until medical help arrived, Beattie raced down to the forecastle and helped direct the evacuation of the wounded. He knew the listing ship was in extreme danger of capsizing as the USS *Oklahoma* did.

Hope of saving the *West Virginia* from a similar fate rested in the hands of Lieutenant Claude Ricketts, Lieutenant Commander John Harper, and several ensigns who began counterflooding measures. The men were sprinting throughout the bottom of the ship, opening valves to allow seawater to rush into starboard voids and compartments on the opposite side of the torpedoed holes, trying to level the vessel.

Back on the bridge, Chief Pharmacist's Mate Leslie Leak, clutching his first-aid kit, arrived along with several officers. One look at the captain's wound and Leak knew immediately that it was fatal. He placed a bandage over the abdomen and gave the captain a shot of morphine to ease the pain.

A skipper who cared greatly about the welfare of his men, Bennion noticed that Radioman 1st Class John Glass, who was assisting Leak, was bleeding badly from a gash in his lip. The captain told Leak, "Don't worry any more about me. Take care of him." After Glass was treated, the captain ordered him to go below and help close watertight doors and hatches.

Ricketts arrived on the bridge and told Bennion that the counterflooding had been successful although it meant that several unfortunate sailors were trapped in flooded compartments with no chance of escape or rescue. "The ship is leveling out and won't turn turtle on us," Ricketts reported. "She will sink into the mud and settle, but the water shouldn't reach any higher than the main deck."

"Well, that's something to be thankful for," the skipper rasped. If Bennion knew he was dying, he didn't say a word about it. Although he was gasping between each sentence and his voice was growing weaker, the strong-minded captain disregarded his agony and continued to issue orders. He conferred with the officers about the condition of the ship, the evacuation of the wounded, and the danger of the fires spreading across the decks. Hearing that it was impossible to fire the portside guns and that the portside magazines were flooded, Bennion ordered one of the ensigns, "Send the A-A [antiaircraft] gun crews to the *Tennessee* to assist in return fire."

"Captain, we need to move you," said Ricketts, keeping a wary eye on the attacking planes that were buzzing above and the fires that were flaring on the ship's deck below. "It's not safe here on the bridge."

"No, I am staying," Bennion replied. "This is where a skipper remains when he's trying to save his ship."

To make him more comfortable, sailors brought out a cot and carefully lifted the skipper and set him on it. The pain grew worse, but Bennion kept asking for updates.

"Everyone is doing everything possible to fight the fires and control the damage," Ricketts assured him.

But the smoke and flames were creeping closer to the bridge, prompting Ricketts to say, "Sir, it's getting too dangerous here."

"Leave me, all of you, and save yourselves," Bennion wheezed. "That's an order."

"Captain, we will not abandon you," Ricketts countered.

*　　*　　*

In the blackness, Cole was trembling in terror. The hatches in front were dogged and water was pouring in from behind. He had nowhere to go. His mind was seized with thoughts of death by drowning. The seasoned sailors—the old salts—had warned him that if the ship were ever sinking, seamen faced the danger of being caught on the wrong side of a dogged area and drowned like rats. "If you're ever trapped like that," a longtime seaman had told Cole shortly after the swabby arrived on the *West Virginia*, "just inhale water quickly and get it over with 'cause it beats dyin' a slow death in the dark."

Suddenly, Cole heard a series of tremendous bangs that rattled the ship and momentarily stunned him. To his surprise, he saw a shaft of light beaming down through a small ragged opening overhead several feet away. And then he noticed what caused it—a bomb. It had crashed through the main deck, penetrated the other decks, and stopped in the twisted metal of the smoky compartment that he was in.

It's a dud! Thank God, it's a dud! Had it exploded, he would have been vaporized. But he was alive because, amazingly, it hadn't detonated. In an ironic twist of fate that wasn't lost on Cole, the enemy had just given him the opportunity to escape from certain death.

He scrambled over the rubble until he was directly underneath the hole, which was barely wide enough for him to squeeze through. Petty Officer Bill White, who had been searching for the wounded in the deck above, peered down through the hole and spotted Cole. "This is the way out," White said. He extended his hand in the opening, grasped Cole's, and yanked him out and into a berthing compartment where several sailors were lying unconscious.

"Help get these men out of here," White told him. "Water is coming in." He pointed to a passageway and said, "That'll lead you to the main deck. I'm going to look for other survivors."

The person closest to Cole was a large sailor sprawled at the base of a hatch. Cole kneeled down and turned him over. In the dim light he recognized the face. *It's Doris!*

He shook Miller, but his friend remained unconscious. "Come on, Doris, wake up! Wake up! The ship is sinking. We've got to get out of here."

Cole glanced around for someone to help him lift Miller, but there was no one. *I'm going to have to do this myself,* he thought. *Am I strong enough?* The sailor somehow found the strength to drape his 235-pound shipmate—who weighed 55 pounds more than Cole—on his shoulders and staggered up to the main deck.

Enemy planes were still bombing and strafing ships when Cole stumbled forward with his heavy load to a casualty collection point, where corpsmen were treating the wounded. Leaving his unconscious friend in the care of others, Cole thought, *Where did I find the strength to carry him?*

When Miller regained consciousness, his head ached, but he was otherwise all right. Seeing wounded being carried to the forecastle and put onto boats, Miller once again began bringing the injured out from belowdecks. It wasn't easy because of the list and the sloshing, oily water that made the footing slick.

After retrieving another injured sailor, Miller was stopped by Lieutenant Commander Doir Johnson, the ship's communications officer, at "Times Square," a central spot on the ship where the main fore-to-aft and port-to-starboard passageways crossed.

"Miller, you're just the man I need," Johnson said. "Come with me. The captain is on the bridge, badly wounded. I need your help to carry him down."

Arriving on the bridge, Miller saw the captain in full uniform lying on a cot, his midsection dark red with blood. Although there was a letup in the attack, the onboard fires were fanning out over the ship. "It's time to get the skipper out of here," Ricketts said.

Following Ricketts's orders, Miller and Lieutenant Frederick White—a tall, strong officer nicknamed "Snowshoes" because of his size 14EEE shoes—picked up the cot and carried the skipper to a ladder that led down from the signal bridge. They intended to bring him to the main deck below and then transfer him to a rescue boat. But because the captain was a large, heavyset man, the cot sagged and almost broke, so the plan was scrapped. Miller and White moved him from an exposed position to a sheltered spot behind the conning tower.

Then another wave of enemy planes roared over the

harbor, launching the second half of the fierce attack. A Zero flew by, firing away at the other side of the conning tower where sailors were manning the No. 1 and No. 2 .50-caliber anti-aircraft machine guns.

Ensign Victor Delano rushed over to Ricketts and reported that the gunners had been killed. Ricketts told Delano, "You and White take over Numbers One and Two." Turning to Miller, he added, "You load the guns."

Miller had never been allowed to touch such a weapon because of his skin color. But race was no longer an issue. He was pleased he'd have the chance to fight back. White, meanwhile, had loaded ammunition belts into both guns and began firing No. 1.

Because Delano became distracted while moving the dead gunners out of the way, Miller hopped behind the No. 2 gun and started shooting. Even though he had no previous experience, he had some understanding of how to fire it because he had carefully watched gunners manning the weapons during training exercises. He felt confident, having developed a shooter's eye on the farm. But that was when he was firing his .22 rifle at squirrels and small game, not as he was now, manning a .50-caliber machine gun at moving targets that were trying to kill him and his shipmates.

Fearlessly, Miller fired his weapon, moving it on its stationary swivel left, right, and higher at the diving, swooping Japanese planes. He and White unleashed their rounds, trying to thwart the enemy pilots from pressing their attack on the

West Virginia. Although the pair peppered several Zeros, the gunners couldn't bring one down.

About ten minutes into the second attack, Miller fired at a dive-bomber. The plane's engine coughed, then caught fire, spun out of control, and crashed on the other side of Ford Island. "I think I got one!" Miller crowed. "I think I got one!"

After running through all their ammo, Miller, White, and Delano began coughing from the heavy smoke ballooning from the fires raging below. They hustled back to the other side of the conning tower, where Ricketts told them, "We must move the captain and get out ourselves, or we'll be nothing but ashes."

Ricketts had obtained an eight-foot-long wooden ladder to use for transporting Bennion, who was barely conscious. The men lashed the captain to the ladder and tied a line on each corner of it. Miller and White were ready to lower him over the side of the conning tower down to the boat deck. But smoke had enveloped the bridge and boat deck, making it impossible for the seamen to breathe or see beyond a foot or two. The heat was so intense they feared their clothes would burst into flames. They had to back away.

Ricketts had a knife and used it to cut the captain's lines loose from the ladder. Holding their breath, Miller and White picked up the skipper and hauled him to the starboard side of the navigation bridge, where the smoke wasn't quite so bad.

Bennion was slipping in and out of consciousness. In one barely lucid moment, he whispered with great effort that he was proud of his officers and crew for their conduct during the treacherous attack.

By this time, the fire had spread to the life jacket storage area under the bridge, and flames were coming up through parts of that deck. Then the signal flags caught on fire. Although their hands were becoming singed, Miller, White, and Ricketts threw the burning flags over the side. Leaving Leak with the captain, the rest of the men focused on fighting the fire.

On the main deck, Ensign Hank Graham looked up and saw, through the smoke, that the men on the bridge were in peril. He dashed to the starboard boat crane and climbed it. From there, he tossed them a heaving line and secured his end to a fire hose, which they pulled to the bridge. The hose was connected to a fire plug on the *Tennessee*. White, Miller, and Ricketts turned on the hose, hoping to knock down the blaze on the forward part of the bridge, but the water pressure was not strong enough to emit an effective stream. Other sailors under Graham's direction were trying to stamp out the fire on the boat deck directly below the bridge.

While the men on the bridge continued their futile attempt to squelch the fire, Leak went up to Ricketts and said, "Sir, the captain is dead."

Ricketts sighed and said, "The captain was noble to the very end." Turning his attention to the lives of his men, he added, "We can't do him any good staying here. We need to go."

Graham, who was 50 feet away, tossed the men another line that he tied to the crane while they secured their end to the flag bridge. Leaving the body of the captain behind, they went hand over hand on the rope to the crane and descended to the deck. There, they joined others in fighting the fires in the starboard casemates.

After dropping off Miller at the casualty collection point, Cole looked aft at the blazing *Arizona* and then fore at the over-turned hull of the *Oklahoma*. Cole thought, *The harbor looks like a horror movie.*

Peering through curling clouds of smoke that had drifted over the *West Virginia,* he was surprised that the American flag was not flying off the stern as it should have been. Then he realized why. Flag-raising always occurred at 8 A.M. The attack began five minutes before that.

It's my duty to find a flag and fly it, he told himself. His father had taught him early in childhood of the important symbolism Old Glory represented. And the navy had reinforced that notion. *If ever there's a need to fly the flag, it's now.*

Cole hurried to the bunting locker and pulled out the big-gest flag he could find. He carried it past the flames to the 20-foot flagstaff that angled outward off the stern. Noticing that most of the halyard had been burned off, he thought, *How am I going to hoist the flag?*

Then he saw rope dangling off the pulley at the end of the pole. *I'll use that,* he thought. Even though Zeros were still strafing Battleship Row, and the blazing *Arizona* 50 feet away was radiating severe heat, Cole tucked the flag under his arm and began shinnying up the four-inch-thick flagstaff.

His eyes tearing from the inferno in front of him, he unfurled the flag and attached the top end to what was left of the burned halyard. Then he clutched the bottom part of the flag and scooted back down to the stern and secured it to the base of the flagstaff.

Against the background of the boiling black smoke, the Stars and Stripes proudly stood out, waving in defiance. Amid the din of war that was reverberating across the harbor, Cole could hear some of his shipmates giving the flag a cheer.

For the rest of the morning and into the early afternoon, Cole fought fires on his ship, which had settled on the bottom of the shallow harbor with water lapping over the sides of the main deck. Among the last sailors to leave the *West Virginia*, he took one final look aft. The American flag was still flying.

After escaping from the smoky bridge, Miller joined shipmates in beating back the flames. But with little water pressure, it was futile. She would have to burn out on her own. They abandoned ship.

Early that afternoon, the exhausted seaman made it to a barrack on shore. Miller knew that his folks back home would be worried sick, wondering if he was among the injured or dead. So he sat down and wrote them a letter—one that didn't mention a word about his heroism on the *West Virginia*. He ended the letter by writing, "Mother, don't worry about me, and tell my friends not to shed any tears for me, for when the dark clouds pass over, I'll be back on the sunny side."

Of the 1,541 men on the West Virginia *during the attack, 106 were killed and 52 were wounded. The battleship was eventually refloated and repaired and went back into battle.*

Captain Bennion was posthumously awarded the Medal of Honor for "conspicuous devotion to duty, extraordinary courage, and complete disregard of his own life, above and beyond the call of duty, during the attack on the Fleet in Pearl Harbor."

Five months after the attack, Doris Miller became the first African American to receive the Navy Cross. He was presented the medal for extraordinary courage under fire by Admiral Chester W. Nimitz, the commander in chief for the Pacific Fleet. During the ceremony, which took place aboard the aircraft carrier USS Enterprise, *the admiral noted, "This marks the first time in this conflict that such high tribute has been made in the Pacific Fleet to a member of his race, and I'm sure that the future will see others similarly honored for brave acts."*

A month earlier, the navy had formally abolished its ban on African Americans holding any rank above steward or messman. Miller was one of the first black sailors to be featured on a navy recruiting poster.

He continued to serve in the Pacific and was eventually transferred to the escort carrier the USS Liscome Bay, *where he held* the rank of Cook 3rd class. On November 24, 1943, during the Battle of Tarawa in the South Pacific, a torpedo from a Japanese submarine struck the Liscome Bay, detonating the ship's bomb magazine. Within a few minutes, the vessel sank, claiming the lives of 646 of her 918 sailors. Among the dead was Doris Miller.

Paying tribute to his sacrifice and heroism, the navy named a new destroyer escort after him in 1973, and in 2010 the United States Postal Service released a commemorative stamp with his likeness as part of its "distinguished sailors" series. Schools, housing projects, parks, and memorials have been named in his honor.

Arles Cole served as a sailor on several ships throughout the rest of the war under mostly battle conditions. Afterward, he served as an advocate for fellow veterans in their dealings with veterans' governmental programs. He wrote an autobiography called Showing Our Colors at Pearl Harbor: A Firsthand Account through the Eyes of a 17-Year-Old Survivor. As of 2015, Cole was still speaking to groups and schools about patriotism and the sacrifices made by men and women of the United States military.

Claude Ricketts became a four-star admiral in the navy and served as vice chief of naval operations. Victor Delano and Frederick White served throughout the Pacific and were eventually promoted to captain.

THE DEATH TRAP

Heroes of the USS *Utah*

After the USS *Utah* was struck by two devastating torpedoes, she began to list so badly and quickly to port, the crew was ordered to abandon ship immediately. She was doomed.

As the thick hawsers that had been keeping the vessel from capsizing began snapping in two from the strain, the sailors knew they had mere seconds to escape before she flipped over. They jumped overboard or slid down the rolling hull.

Several decks down, Peter Tomich and Jack Vaessen refused to leave when ordered. Even though they knew the ship would capsize at any moment and thwart most any chance of escape, they remained at their posts, doing what they were trained to do, so that others could live. Each second that ticked by brought the two sailors that much closer to their deaths. They knew there was no time left. They had to leave *now*!

But then, with a big splash and loud gurgle, the *Utah* turned turtle.

I waited too long, thought Vaessen.

*   *   *

The *Utah* was the oldest of the nine battleships moored at Pearl Harbor. After serving for 23 years as a warship, including during World War 1, she had been turned into a target ship in 1931. For years, pilots from the army, navy, and Marine Corps had dropped nonexplosive practice bombs on her decks, which had been covered with two layers of 6-inch-by-12-inch timbers for protection.

After nine weeks at sea getting "bombed," the *Utah* returned to Pearl Harbor on Thursday, December 4, and tied up at a quay off of the west side of Ford Island. Battleship Row was on the east side. She was scheduled to have the wood taken away Monday and then sail to California. To prepare for the removal, the crew spent Friday and Saturday lifting up the lumber and stacking it in eight-foot-high piles on the main deck.

Shortly before 8 A.M. Sunday, the first torpedo struck the *Utah* amidships on the port side and was followed a minute later by the second torpedo. They blasted giant holes through her fuel tanks, sending seawater and oil surging into her compartments and causing her to list almost immediately.

The *Utah* was completely defenseless because she was still rigged for service as a target ship. Heavy steel sheds known as dog houses covered her big guns to protect them from the dummy bombs. Most of the other weapons, including machine guns, had been dismantled and stowed in storerooms below-decks along with the ammunition, which had been secured in the magazines.

*   *   *

Pharmacist's Mate 2nd Class Lee Soucy, 22, was looking forward to going home. His two-year enlistment period was up on this very day, and he planned to make the rounds and say good-bye to his fellow sailors because he was scheduled to ship out on Monday.

When the *Utah* shuddered from the deafening blast from the initial torpedo strike, Soucy snatched his first-aid bag and dashed toward his battle station amidships. As he was running down the passageway, the second torpedo shook the ship so hard it knocked him off-balance and through the log room door. Rising to his feet in a daze, he staggered down the ladder below the armored deck where several sailors were in shock, asking, "What's going on?"

Soucy felt around his shoulder and yelped in dismay. *My first-aid kit! It's gone. I must have dropped it when I was thrown into the log room.* Before he had a chance to think about retrieving it, he heard the boatswain's whistle and then the order, "All hands on deck! Abandon ship! All hands on deck! Abandon ship!"

Fireman 2nd Class John "Jack" Vaessen had arrived 15 minutes early for his 8 A.M. watch several decks down in the switchboard room, which controlled the ship's electrical system. He was fiddling with a flashlight that wasn't working right when he felt a severe jolt. Then water started pouring into the compartment. At first he thought a ship had accidentally rammed the *Utah*. But when another strong tremor shook her, he was certain she had been bombed or torpedoed. More water cascaded into the compartment, causing batteries to explode.

Running over to the forward distribution board, which supplied all electrical circuits for the front half of the ship, Vaessen noticed that the voltage began dropping and the lights began dimming. He could feel the vessel listing rapidly, and realized the *Utah* was in grave danger of capsizing.

Hearing the order to abandon ship, Vaessen thought, *I can't leave yet. I've got to keep the lights on so the crewmen can find their way out.* He cut power to all nonessential circuits to maintain lights in the ship as long as possible. Even though he wished he could flee, too, he felt duty bound to remain at his post. *The longer the lights can stay on,* he figured, *the more men will be saved.* Running back and forth between the fore and aft distribution boards, the switch-flipping seaman kept vital passageways lit in the interior of the vessel.

Others were just as determined to help their fellow crewmen escape. In the ship's central station, Electrician's Mate 2nd Class George Hettinger stayed at his post at another distribution board, constantly replacing fuses that kept blowing out so that the passageways could remain illuminated. Hearing the order to abandon ship, Hettinger assisted several men up ladders that were becoming increasingly hard to scale because of the severe angle of the *Utah*'s tilt. By directing a human chain of outstretched arms, he helped a dozen sailors topside.

* * *

Deep inside the *Utah*, Chief Water Tender Peter Tomich, who was in charge of the ship's engine and boiler rooms, stumbled from the back-to-back torpedo strikes. As the bulkheads began to buckle and the water gushed into the lower compartments, he hurried in the opposite direction of sailors who were scrambling up toward the main deck. He reached his battle station in the port engine room where his men were working in rising knee-deep water. They reported that steam had dropped and the drain pumps wouldn't start. The starboard engine room was also flooding.

Seeing the water swirling toward the hot boilers that powered the ship, Tomich realized they could rupture and explode, possibly killing everyone onboard. His primary concern—his only concern—was the safety of the entire crew, especially the men who worked directly under his supervision. They were his brothers, and he loved them; he had no close family of his own.

Tomich was born Petar Tonic in 1893 in the small Balkan village of Prolog, in what is now the country of Bosnia-Herzegovina. When he was 20, he immigrated to the United States. As was often the case with immigrants who entered the country through Ellis Island, his name was either deliberately or accidentally changed. Petar Tonic became Peter Tomich. He stayed in New York with his cousin John Tonic, who had immigrated with him.

When America entered World War I in 1917, Tomich enlisted in the US Army. While serving his adopted country, he applied for and received American citizenship. After his 18-month stint ended and he was honorably discharged, he decided to make a career in the military. So ten days later, he joined the US Navy.

Tomich gained a reputation as a solid, caring sailor who became one of the most experienced water tenders of the entire Pacific Fleet, having 22 years of service under his belt. No one had a better working knowledge of the pipes, gauges, and valves in the engine and boiler rooms than the 48-year-old water tender did. Although it was a thankless, demanding job, he relished it and the men he worked with.

Now as he saw the looming possibility of a deadly, catastrophic explosion from the huge boilers, he ordered those around him, "Get out! Get out now!" He didn't need anyone to tell him that there was no way to prevent the *Utah* from capsizing. "Get topside!" he shouted. "Go! Go! The ship is turning over! You have to escape now!"

Although she was listing badly and many of her compartments were flooded, the lights remained on, thanks to Vaessen's efforts. Once on deck, the sailors had three choices: jump off the vessel, slide down the exposed hull, or go hand over hand along the groaning hawsers that were stretched rigid to the mooring quays. But abandoning ship was far from safe. The enemy planes that had finished their initial attack runs were now strafing the crippled *Utah*. The planes' concentrated, heavy machine gun fire was savagely cutting down sailors who were leaping off the ship, working their way along the hawsers, or swimming toward Ford Island.

Increasing the peril, the timbers that had been protecting the ship now turned into deadly hazards. Because of the severe list, the unsecured lumber that had been stacked for offloading for the following day began to tumble onto the main deck. The falling timber landed on several unlucky seamen, pinning them or crushing their limbs. Some of the wood slid over hatches and jammed doors, making it impossible for those crewmen on the other side to get out.

Even those who had left the ship still faced dangers. Some couldn't swim; others floundered in the water from swallowing oil and seawater. A few were seriously injured when timbers rolled off the ship and struck them. Those fortunate enough to get picked up by small rescue boats discovered that the vessels made tempting targets for the strafing planes.

The engine room was empty now except for one lone figure— Tomich. His men had scurried up the ladders to the main deck, thinking that he was right behind them. But he had ignored his own orders to flee because he was the only person who could prevent the boilers from blowing up. He hustled from valve to valve and gauge to gauge, methodically working in the proper sequence, releasing steam and shutting down and securing the huge boilers. He had to get it all done in time to prevent a blast that would kill hundreds of shipmates.

But he was savvy enough to know the *Utah* would capsize at any moment, and that by remaining in the engine room, he was giving up his only chance of escape.

On the main deck, an officer stood by a pile of life preservers and tossed them at the sailors as they went by on their way to abandoning the listing ship. Grabbing a preserver, Soucy thought, *What about the huge amount of ammunition we have onboard? If water reaches the boilers, they'll surely blow up—and that could happen any time. I need to get off of this ship fast!*

Fearing he would be slowed down by putting on a life jacket, he tossed his away. With the *Utah* nearly on her side, some sailors stepped off the port side into the water, risking getting struck by the rolling timbers. Because Soucy was a good swimmer and diver, he planned to leap over the much higher starboard side and swim to Ford Island, which he estimated to be about 500 to 600 feet away (nearly the length of 2 football fields). But then he remembered that the shoreline along the island was made up of jagged, sharp coral rock. While other sailors were kicking off their shoes before jumping into the water, he tied double knots on his shoes so his feet wouldn't get cut up when he reached the beach.

Just as Soucy was poised to do a running dive off the increasingly exposed hull, the 2-foot-thick mooring lines that had kept the 21,000-ton *Utah* from flipping completely over began snapping one by one like whips lashing through the air.

Sailors who had been escaping hand over hand on the hawsers were flung into the water.

The ship lurched, throwing everybody who was standing on the side of the hull off-balance. Like so many others, Soucy lost his footing from the sudden jerk and landed on his rear. Then he went sliding down the rough, barnacle-encrusted hull, cutting up his buttocks and hands, unable to grasp at anything to slow him down. He skidded off the hull and plunged into the water.

The ship shuddered as if it had been struck again and then rolled over with a loud splash until its masts dug into the muddy floor of the harbor. From the time the *Utah* was first torpedoed to when she went belly-up, it took only 11 minutes.

As the ship turned turtle, the lights inside her dimmed and finally went out for good. Vaessen grabbed his flashlight and a wrench. Hanging on to whatever he could grasp to keep his balance, Vaessen was smacked by loose deck plates, fire extinguishers, and electrical equipment. As water gushed into the compartment, he struggled to keep his composure. He quickly figured out that there was no escaping topside because topside was now at the bottom.

Rather than panic, Vaessen realized that his only chance to survive was to be rescued. That meant he had to find his way to a void and reach the bottom of the hull—which was above him—and make a lot of noise in the hopes that people outside would hear him and cut him out of the capsized ship.

Orienting himself to this new and frightening upside-down world, Vaessen sloshed through the dynamo room and into a workshop, where he found a manhole cover to the bilge compartment over his head. Using his wrench, he loosened the manhole's bolts and opened the cover. He climbed up and into the ship's bottom and began banging away on the inside of the hull with his wrench while shouting for help.

Until the bitter end, Lieutenant Commander Solomon Isquith, the senior officer onboard at the time of the attack, kept up a steady stream of orders as he directed the seamen to abandon their capsizing ship. Only when she finally flipped on her side did he try to leave.

Escape was through one of the portholes, which were now above him. But because he was heavyset, he couldn't fit through the regular portholes. However, there was a larger one in the captain's cabin. As water began filling the room, Isquith climbed onto the captain's bed to reach the porthole and open it. The bed collapsed, but Lieutenant Commander Lindley Winser, the radio chief, and a mess attendant named Simmons, who were both on the other side of the porthole, each grabbed one of Isquith's hands and pulled him to safety.

Moments later, Winser swam away from the ship, climbed aboard a small motorboat, and took command of it. His boat and two other rescue boats circled the hull, braving the strafing planes, to pick up sailors who had jumped overboard. The boats transported the survivors to Ford Island, where all hands were ordered into trenches that had recently been dug for an unfinished sewer project. The trenches provided decent cover for the sailors from the strafing and bombing.

When Soucy bobbed to the surface, he saw that the Utah had keeled over. The sight left him too stunned to think of anything except his own survival. He spotted a motor launch with a coxswain who was fishing men out of the water with a boat hook. *Oh, good,* Soucy thought. *I won't have to swim for Ford Island.* He began swimming toward the launch, which was filling up with a few dozen sailors who had jumped off the Utah. But after doing a few strokes, Soucy stopped because bullets from a low-flying Zero were hitting the water in front of him and in line with the boat.

The plane is coming back for another strafing run, he told himself. *A boat full of men will be a more desirable target than a lone swimmer.* He changed course and moved away from the boat, diving underwater every time he heard the guns of an enemy plane strafing survivors. Furiously stroking and kicking, Soucy headed for the shoreline, which now seemed miles, rather than 200 yards, away. And as he swam for his life, he wondered, *Can I make it to Ford Island without getting shot?*

Hettinger, the electrician's mate, had jumped off the ship as she capsized and swam to a 20-foot-tall cement mooring quay where several men were perched. They helped him up. But then a bomb exploded nearby and flying shrapnel gored the leg of the sailor next to him.

"Help me!" someone shouted in the water. Hettinger looked down and saw that Fireman 3rd Class Sam Nabors was thrashing around. "I can't swim!" Nabors gurgled before slipping below the surface. Hettinger dived into the water, snared the struggling seaman, and brought him to the quay, where the others lifted both men up. Minutes later, Wisner's boat came by and took the men to shore before it headed back out to rescue more people.

Soucy reached the beach exhausted. While trying to catch his breath, he was shocked by the chaos swirling around him—a sky buzzing with planes, blasts from bombs, eruptions of fireballs, clouds of black smoke, and the screams and shouts of sailors. About the same time, another pharmacist's mate, Gordon Sumner, from the *Utah*, hobbled out of the water.

"Am I ever glad to see you!" Soucy told him.

"Yeah," Sumner replied, breathing heavily. "Misery loves company." He took off the first-aid kit that he had wrapped around his shoulders and plopped down on a rock.

"Geez," said Soucy, "I feel guilty that I lost my first-aid kit and didn't make any effort to recover it. Everything is crazy."

Sumner gestured to their overturned ship. "Pretty sad," he muttered. "It was our home."

"It's like seeing your house go up in flames," Soucy said. "It makes you want to cry."

"At least she didn't explode like I feared."

"I wonder how many are trapped inside and will never get out."

As sailors crouched in the trench along the shore, they began hearing a faint banging noise coming from the overturned hull. "It sounds like men are trapped in there," said Isquith, who had reached Ford Island. He asked for volunteers to investigate. Even though the Japanese were still attacking, Warrant Officer and Machinist Stanley Szymanski, Chief Machinist's Mate Terrance MacSelwiney, and two other sailors hopped into a motor launch and returned to the capsized *Utah*. Avoiding bullets while climbing up the hull, they followed the banging sound. It led them to the forward end of the hull, where they kneeled down above what they figured was a void by the dynamo room. They tapped on the hull and heard a response. "Someone's alive!" Szymanski shouted toward shore. "We'll have to cut him out!" The rescue team left to get the necessary equipment.

Inside the hull, Vaessen pounded furiously with his wrench and then stopped when he heard tapping sounds coming from the outside. *Did I really hear that?* He tapped again and someone tapped back. Vaessen was elated. *They've come to rescue me!* Soon, though, there was nothing but silence. *Did they not hear me? Did the Japs kill them?* After several minutes passed, he thought, *I could die a slow death.*

* * *

A speeding jeep on the beachside road came roaring up to Soucy and Sumner and screeched to a halt. Spotting their Red Cross armbands, the officer in the jeep hollered, "Corpsmen, come with me!" They were taken to a two-story concrete-and-steel bachelor officers' quarters that faced Battleship Row. Inside, about 50 sailors who had swum through the oil-laden, flaming water from the destroyed *Arizona*, *Oklahoma*, and *West Virginia* were sprawled on the concrete floor.

"We need you two to set up an emergency treatment station here," the officer told the corpsmen.

Many of the sailors were vomiting oil or had oil oozing out of their nostrils and the corners of their mouths. Others were bleeding from bullet and shrapnel wounds, and still more were suffering from severe burns. In no time, the supplies in Sumner's bag were exhausted. And more casualties were being brought in by the minute.

"How are you getting along?" the officer asked the corpsmen.

"We've run out of everything and are in urgent need of bandages," Soucy replied.

The officer wheeled around and ordered several men who hadn't been injured, "Strip the beds and make rolls of bandages with the sheets." Turning back to Soucy, "What else?"

"We need some kind of solvent to clean the wounds," Soucy said. "We've been putting iodine on the wounds, but the oil won't let it penetrate to do any good. Rubbing alcohol would be useful."

"Alcohol, huh? Will whiskey do?"

Before Soucy could answer, the officer left and returned minutes later, plunking a case of scotch at the corpsmen's feet. Another soldier who had accompanied him handed them an armful of bottles of gin, bourbon, and vodka. "Will this work?" he asked.

Soucy replied, "I'm sure rubbing alcohol could not serve our purpose any better than this booze."

He and Sumner scurried from one casualty to another, pouring liquor liberally over the oil-covered wounds and burns and then washing off the oil.

At one point, an exhausted sailor dripping from head to toe in oil, stumbled in. Seeing Soucy hustling around with a washcloth in one hand and a bottle of vodka in the other, the sailor shouted, "Hey, Doc, could I have a shot of that 'medicine'?" After Soucy handed him the bottle, the sailor took a hefty swig. As soon as he swallowed the vodka, the sailor threw up mucus blackened by the oil. After he stopped vomiting, he told Soucy, "Doc, I lost that medicine. How about another dose?"

Szymanski's rescue party motored over to the nearby cruiser, the USS *Raleigh*, which was struggling to stay afloat because she had been struck by a torpedo and a bomb. As water lapped over her main deck, Captain Robert Simons provided the rescuers with an acetylene torch, other equipment, and several men to assist them.

With MacSelwiney operating the launch, the half dozen sailors avoided getting strafed and returned to the *Utah*. Disregarding the machine gun fire and falling bombs, the crew went to work cutting a hole in the hull.

Inside, Vaessen was overjoyed when he heard the rescue party. He kept banging his wrench to alert them that he was still alive. *I'm going to be saved*, he told himself. *That is, if the Japs don't kill them.* Time couldn't go fast enough for him. After 90 minutes, he saw, above his head, a small glowing red spot that grew increasingly larger. Soon sparks from the cutting torch were raining on him, but he didn't care. *This is the best shower I've ever had!*

Finally, shortly after 11 A.M., about three hours after he was trapped, Vaessen was pulled out of the hole in the hull. The rescuers, though, were disheartened to learn he wasn't aware of any other survivors.

Although using booze to treat wounds was not accepted medical practice, it made Soucy popular with the sailors. But in reality, the liquor did its job as a solvent and also induced vomiting, which helped casualties get rid of the contaminated water and oil in their stomachs.

Sumner went in search of medical supplies at the nearby naval dispensary. When he returned with them, he told Soucy, "I almost didn't make it. A bomb landed no more than ten yards away from me."

Soucy shook his head and said, "Come on, if you had been that close, you'd have been killed."

Sumner nodded. "I know. But it didn't go off. It was a dud."

After being relieved from the makeshift treatment center, Soucy walked to the navy hospital, where he worked until 1 A.M. Monday. After catching a few hours of sleep, he started drawing blood and worked another 48 hours around the clock. There was so much to do that there wasn't time for him to ponder the enormity of the Pearl Harbor tragedy.

Burns accounted for about 60 percent of the nearly 1,000 casualties that were treated at the hospital the first day. Many of the injuries were "flash burns" caused by intense heat from exploding bombs. In some of the worst cases, sailors suffered burns over as much as 80 percent of their bodies.

In the ward, a radio was blaring one of the year's most popular songs sung by a male quartet called the Ink Spots. One of the burned sailors who was lying in bed and listening to the song, which was called "I Don't Want to Set the World on Fire," yelled out, "Guys, you're too late. It's done been set!"

Although 461 officers and enlisted men from the Utah *survived the capsizing, 58 sailors perished, most of them trapped inside. Among the dead was Peter Tomich, who gave his life to prevent her from blowing up.*

For his heroic actions, Tomich was posthumously named a recipient of the Medal of Honor, but the navy couldn't find any family members to present them with his medal.

He had listed the next of kin as his cousin John Tonic, of New York City. But Tonic had returned to his native country in 1921. He never knew of Tomich's heroism, and couldn't be found.

The navy decided that the medal belonged on the USS Tomich, a destroyer escort named in his honor. The medal hung in a small passageway forward of the galley of the ship, which saw action during World War II in both the Atlantic and Pacific, mostly escorting convoys.

After the ship was taken out of service in 1946, the medal once again was orphaned. When the governor of Utah, Herbert Maw, learned about it, he proclaimed Tomich an honorary citizen of the state, which was then granted guardianship of the medal. It was displayed in the State House, alongside a memorial to the Utah. Eventually, the navy regained custody of the medal, and in 1989 placed it in the newly built Tomich Hall, the main academic building of the Senior Enlisted Academy in Newport, Rhode Island.

But Rear Admiral J. Robert Lunney felt strongly that the medal belonged with the hero's family. In 1997, he began a personal search at his own expense for Tomich's kin. He traveled to Tomich's hometown of Prolog, where he interviewed villagers and examined church and government records. To his delight, Lunney finally found Tomich's distant relatives.

At a ceremony in 2006 aboard the aircraft carrier USS Enterprise, which was anchored off the coast of Split, Croatia, Tomich's Medal of Honor was presented to retired Croatian Army lieutenant colonel Srecko Herceg Tonic, grandson of the hero's cousin John Tonic.

Lunney and his family were among those who attended the presentation. Lunney said he felt gratified that his efforts paid off but also saddened that "a true naval hero sacrificed his life."

During the ceremony, Admiral Henry Ulrich III, commander of US Naval Forces in Europe, said, "Chief Water Tender Peter Tomich's selfless heroism and steadfast courage represented the very best of his native country and his adopted one as well. A common man became uncommon and left fear aside. Such people we call heroes."

Solomon Isquith was awarded the Navy Cross because, according to the citation, "With extraordinary courage and disregard of his own safety, [he] directed the abandonment of the ship when it was capsizing rapidly, in such a cool and efficient manner that approximately 90 percent of the crew were saved."

John Vaessen was awarded the Navy Cross for keeping the lighting system working so others could escape while the ship was sinking. Stanley Szymanski and Terrance MacSelwiney received Letters of Commendation for their heroic efforts in rescuing Vaessen. George Hettinger also was given a commendation for helping keep the lights on, assisting in the ship's evacuation, and rescuing fellow sailor Sam Nabors.

Of all the ships hit at Pearl Harbor on that fateful day, only the Arizona and the Utah still lie where they sank. An effort to salvage the Utah in 1944 failed, so the vessel was left in the harbor. Today a 40-foot-by-15-foot concrete platform connected to Ford Island by a walkway stands as a memorial to the ship and her crew.

A visit to the USS Utah Memorial requires special approval for nonmilitary personnel to access it.

In 2006, Lee Soucy returned to Pearl Harbor for the sixty-fifth anniversary of the sneak attack. The trip helped heal decades-old emotional wounds after he met a few Japanese pilots who had participated in the raid. "It was a good thing to talk to them," Soucy told reporters later. "You don't want to die with hate in your heart."

Five years later, following Soucy's death at age 90, a navy diver took a small urn containing the corpsman's ashes and placed it in a porthole of the sunken ship in an internment ceremony. Soucy's dying wish was to remain forever with the shipmates he had lost during the attack.

GOING DOWN FIGHTING

Heroes of the USS *California*

When general quarters sounded on the USS *California*, Jackson Pharris, a 29-year-old gunner from Georgia, rushed toward his battle station located three decks down. To reach his post as quickly as possible, he didn't use the ladders. Instead, he jumped through each hatch, grabbing a bar attached to the overhead of the deck below and swung himself into the lower passageway like a trapeze artist.

Just as he entered the compartment where he was in charge of an ordnance repair party, a torpedo struck almost directly under him. The impact hurled Pharris upward, slamming him so hard against the overhead that it nearly knocked him out. Seconds later, the ship shook again from a second torpedo strike. His head pounding from an instant headache and his body bruised from the battering it took, the dazed sailor needed a few minutes to recover.

The first torpedo had peeled open a 40-foot-wide gash on

the port side and the other created a 27-foot-wide hole and ruptured the ship's fuel tanks. Seawater and oil poured into the third deck, knocking out much of the ship's power, lights, and pumps. The *California* began listing to port.

The explosions had destroyed the machinery—the hoists and conveyer belts—that supplied the ammunition to the guns. Rather than wait for orders, Pharris decided to act. "We need to set up a hand-supply ammunition train for the A-A guns," he told his shipmates. He had them line up from the entrance to the magazine all the way to the closest big guns and hand ammo from one person to another.

But before they could start the human chain, a bomb exploded on the bow, rocking the ship. Once again, Pharris was lifted off his feet and whacked against the bulkhead, as were his shipmates. The force of the blast twisted the bulkhead so badly that rivets popped out and flew across the compartment like bullets.

Bleeding, hurt, and in shock, Pharris lay crumpled on the floor. He regained his senses and realized that if action wasn't taken immediately, the ship would capsize. Even though he was of much lower rank than the officers who were topside, Pharris found several shipfitters and ordered them to counterflood compartments on the starboard side, which, if done right, would balance out the vessel and keep it from turning over. Knowing the *California* was in crisis mode, they didn't wait to hear directly from an officer.

"We'll keep her on an even keel if we work fast enough," a shipfitter told Pharris. "But there's nothing we can do to stop her from sinking."

"Don't let her capsize or too many sailors will die," Pharris said. Ignoring the pain that racked his entire body, he returned to his main task, directing a human chain to feed ammo to the antiaircraft guns.

Chief Radioman Thomas Reeves felt the *California* shudder badly from the two torpedo blasts, but the Connecticut-born 45-year-old career navy man stayed focused on his job in the radio room below the third deck. When water started cascading into the compartment, an officer ordered Reeves to evacuate and secure the door behind him.

After carrying out the order, Reeves joined the human chain of ammo handlers under Pharris's direction on the third deck. By now, the oil gushing from the damaged fuel tanks was creating noxious fumes that, mixed with the smoke in the interior, only grew stronger. The hot, lung-searing smoke began choking the sailors in the passageway, where Reeves urged his shipmates around him to hang tough. Even as some of them began faltering and passing out, he told the others, "We can't leave the A-A guns without ammo. Keep going!"

But more men were losing consciousness until the human chain was broken. Soon, as one of the few who were still try-ing to lug rounds through the corridor, Reeves could no longer tolerate the heat or the fumes and collapsed into unconsciousness.

Pharris, who was farther away from the source of the smoke and fire, shouted to those who were barely able to stand, "Let's get the men who've fallen out of here!" Going deeper into the passageway, he, too, was finding it difficult to breathe and began gagging until he became faint. As he reached down to pick up an unconscious shipmate, Pharris dropped to his knees and passed out. When he regained consciousness, he dragged the sailor to safety.

Every breath Pharris took hurt, and every muscle he moved triggered intense pain. But he willed himself to disregard the agony because other seamen who had passed out would die if they weren't rescued. Adding to the threat, the deck was flooding badly.

The only good news: The severe listing had stopped and the ship was righting herself. The counterflooding had worked.

Holding his breath, Pharris began hauling out unconscious victims one at a time. Each time he dragged a seaman out of the passageway, he handed him off to another sailor who took him topside.

Entering a compartment that was knee-deep in oil, Pharris discovered an unconscious shipmate who was drowning in the fuel. The gunner picked him up and threw him over his shoulder. Staggering down the passageway on wobbly knees, Pharris was breathing heavily and sucked in too much of the fumes and passed out for the second time.

Once again, he regained consciousness and brought the sailor to safety. Pharris's stirring example of heroism inspired the men around him not to panic. Rather than blindly flee from the flooding and suffocating fumes, they followed his lead and searched for fellow shipmates on their way topside.

But because the lights were out and the smoke was thick, several seamen weren't found in time. They died where they fell. Reeves was one of them.

Despite the severe damage that the *California* had suffered, the antiaircraft guns were blasting away continuously. In all the chaos, Boatswain's Mate 1st Class William Fleming, 25, a gun captain on one of the batteries, calmly directed his crew.

What his comrades didn't know was his stomach was twisted in knots from worry over his wife and four-year-old son, who were at home just a few miles away in Honolulu. Fleming battled hard within himself to concentrate solely on defending his ship.

"Look out for the Zero!" a sailor shouted.

The fighter roared over the *California*, firing its cannon into the ship. Fleming was struck in the arm and chest with such force, he fell down. Bleeding badly, he tore off part of his uniform and used it as a bandage. Then he went about his job as if nothing had happened, despite the intense pain. Toughing it out, the gun captain kept directing his crew.

*   *   *

Far belowdecks, Machinist's Mate 1st Class Robert Scott, 26, of Massillon, Ohio, was one of the men who kept the air compressors working so the guns could function. It was an undervalued job, but a necessary one. He knew that if the compressors shut down, the guns would, too, because the compressors supplied the guns with jets of air that cleared the barrels after each fired round.

When water and fuel oil began filling the forward air-compressor compartment, the toxic fumes caused the sailors inside to hack and gag. Eventually, when they couldn't stand it any longer, an officer told them to leave. All but Scott sloshed their way out of the room. He remained at his post to keep the guns firing.

Getting woozier by the second, Gunner's Mate 3rd Class Vernon Jensen called out to Scott from the doorway, "Robert, everyone has been ordered to leave their stations now! Come on!"

Scott shook his head. "I'm stayin'," he said. "This is my station."

"But, Robert, it's getting hard to breathe in here, and the water keeps coming up."

"As long as the men are firin' their guns, they're gonna need air. I'm stickin'."

"Robert, please! You'll drown!"

"Shut the door on your way out. Go!"

Jensen, barely able to stand up as the fumes nearly overtook him, closed the door and lurched his way through the rising water to safety. The guns kept going for several more minutes and then fell silent. Jensen knew then he would never see his brave buddy again.

Marine Private Arthur Senior was near the front of an ammunition chain of sailors in a darkened compartment, working furiously under the direction of Ensign Herbert Jones. Although Jones was a fun-loving California native, he took his role in the navy seriously, having followed in his father's footsteps by enlisting in 1935 at the age of 17. Jones became an officer in 1940 and had married his sweetheart shortly before the *California* weighed anchor for Pearl Harbor. Because of his quick wit and warm personality, his shipmates considered him one of their favorite officers.

Now they were following his every command. And as the fumes from the leaking fuel grew stronger, the men in the third deck followed Jones's lead and passed ammo hand to hand as fast as they could.

Among the men in the group was a troublemaking Marine, Private Howard Haynes, who had been in the brig for one too many fights and was awaiting a bad-conduct discharge. But because the ship needed every available hand, Jones released Haynes, saying, "You've shown little or no respect for anything or anyone. Well, here's your chance to change." Haynes nodded and joined the human chain.

For more than a half hour, Jones's group helped keep the guns above firing at the enemy. But then a dive-bomber released a bomb that penetrated the first and second decks and exploded. Senior, like the others, was bowled over. Acrid smoke began filling the compartment, and fire broke out.

"Mr. Jones has been hit!" someone shouted.

Senior grabbed a flashlight and aimed it at the ensign. In the light, the men around him could see that Jones's face and hands were burned and his white uniform was covered in blood. He was barely conscious but had enough strength to gesture that he wanted to be left alone. Senior refused. "We need to move him," the Marine said to his comrades.

He and a sailor started to lug Jones away. Gritting his teeth from the pain, Jones muttered, "Don't carry me any farther."

"But, Mr. Jones . . ."

"I order you to leave me alone," Jones said, gasping for breath. "I'm done for. Get out of here before the magazines go off."

Suddenly, an explosion from the deck below hit with such force that it jolted everyone in the compartment senseless. When Senior regained consciousness a few minutes later, Jones was gone.

At a third deck hatch, Lieutenant Junior Grade Gerald Reese and his gun crew encountered Jones, who had struggled up the ladder from below. Although the two were good friends, Reese could barely recognize the ensign because he was so badly charred and bloody. *He looks like a well-done human hamburger,* thought Reese, hoping his own expression didn't betray the shock he felt at seeing his friend in such horrendous condition.

Jones fell into his arms and in a raspy voice, told him, "Reese, you can't go down there."

"But we have to go below to bring up the ammo for the guns."

His breathing labored, Jones repeated, "Do not . . . go down . . . there."

Reese and two other sailors carried Jones away from the hatch and laid him on a pile of canvas, where he passed out again. Looking into the hatch, Reese winced. "It's a blast furnace down there," he told the others. "Too much smoke and fire."

He kneeled next to Jones to say something to him, but sighed instead. His friend was dead. Realizing there was no time to mourn because the enemy was still attacking, Reese stood up and told his gun crew, "Jones is right. We can't go down there. We'll be of more use on the guns. Let's go back."

Reese and his men eventually took command of an anti-aircraft gun on the starboard side and, thanks to the human chains below, had enough ammo to shoot at the raiders. Firing tracer bullets, he and his gun crew whooped and hollered when they scored a hit on a dive-bomber. The plane burst into flames and broke in half, crashing on the far side of Ford Island.

On the first deck, Haynes scurried over to Second Lieutenant Clifford Drake and said, "I'm alive because of Ensign Jones. I'll do anything to help the crew and this ship. Just give me the chance to prove I'm worth it."

"Start rescuing everybody you can from the fire," Drake replied. "And when you're done, help the others knock down the flames."

Ensign Thomas McGrath stood on the signal bridge, swearing a blue streak and firing his pistol every time a plane strafed the *California*.

But then he learned that several men were trapped in a compartment below central station, deep in the ship where the decks were filling up with seawater and fuel. "We have to find a way to save them," he said.

Knowing that every second counted, McGrath told Chief Yeoman S. R. Miller, "Get me a line and lower me through the trunk [a vertical shaft] to central station."

"But the oil fumes are so strong," Miller said. "You'll pass out."

"It's worth the risk."

After a rope was obtained, Miller and another sailor lowered McGrath into the shaft. Just as Miller feared, the fumes were making McGrath sick and light-headed the farther down he went. Holding his breath for long periods of time, McGrath reached the top of central station's compartment and, with a tool he was carrying, knocked on it. He heard a response from below.

They're still conscious, he told himself. But McGrath was struggling to stay conscious himself, so he signaled to the men above the shaft to pull him up. When he was hauled to the bridge, he gasped for fresh air and rubbed his stinging eyes. After a coughing jag, he told Miller, "We might be able to rescue them by cutting a hole through the deck to central station. But we have to act fast because it will soon be flooded with oil."

Minutes later, McGrath and a volunteer rescue party—armed with an acetylene cutting torch and other equipment—descended down the shaft to the top of central station and began the work of opening a hole. But the fumes were only getting worse, complicating the dire situation. The threat of a flash fire increased as leaking fuel oil crawled closer and closer to them.

The fumes were choking the rescuers. The sailor who was cutting the hole passed out and was replaced by another one who could barely breathe. McGrath and the others were on the verge of losing consciousness, but they still hammered and chiseled until finally they created a big enough hole in the compartment. As water began pouring into central station, the rescue party pulled out all five trapped men.

A petty officer in another part of the ship asked for volunteers to look for survivors in a severely damaged compartment.

"I'll go," said John McGoran, 19, a striker signalman. He and a friend named Smitty arrived at the compartment and found several bodies. A barely alive shipmate, whose eyes were rolled back, was leaning against a bulkhead, slowly slipping to the floor, unconscious.

The two seamen lifted the wounded sailor's limp body and brought him out into the passageway. It was then that McGoran recognized the victim—one of the most unlikable men on the *California*. "If this were yesterday and you asked me to help this offensive guy, I'd have answered, 'To hell with him,'" McGoran told Smitty. "I've known him since boot camp, and he's one of the most overbearing persons I've ever met. But now he's a life to be saved."

Carrying him by his arms and legs, the two sailors had to stop and lay him down several times to catch their breath and to open and close the watertight bulkhead doors. When they reached a ladder that led to a hatch to the upper deck, Smitty took the injured sailor's legs and started up while McGoran held him under the arms. Just as McGoran took the third step up the ladder, another explosion, more powerful than the first two, rocked the ship.

A bomb had penetrated the decks above and exploded in front of the ship's store, several feet forward of the ladder the two shipmates were on, instantly killing dozens of sailors. Somehow, McGoran and Smitty held on to the ladder as well as their unconscious comrade as hot smoke swirled around them. They then carried the seaman to the ship's recreation room, which had been turned into a first-aid station—one in turmoil.

Corpsmen were dashing here and there, treating screaming, moaning men who were suffering from burns, gashes, and broken limbs. Scorched and bloodied bodies were lying in an adjoining room.

A chief petty officer came over to McGoran, pointed to the wounded sailor that McGoran and Smitty had just brought in, and asked gruffly, "Dead or alive?"

"He's alive, Chief," McGoran replied.

"Well, get him out of the way. Slide him under the table, where nobody will trip over him." (The sailor had suffered a broken back.) Then the chief petty officer turned away and told other sailors who were arriving with casualties, "Over here if they're alive. If they're dead, take them into the other room and put them with the rest of the bodies." He made a sweep of the room, inspecting the casualties. Pointing to a lifeless burn victim, he told a mess attendant who was helping out, "This man is dead. Get him out of here."

McGoran wanted to resent the chief petty officer's cold, tough manner, but instead felt only admiration for the man's efficiency in such trying circumstances.

Meanwhile, the ship's doctor, Commander Jesse Jewell, who had suffered burns on his face and arms while fighting a fire at his battle station, was busy administering first aid to the wounded. Despite his own pain and discomfort, he waved off any help from corpsmen so he could concentrate on those who were worse off than him.

As McGoran stood still, trying to comprehend all that had happened in the last hour, someone handed him a bottle of root beer and a sandwich. Ordinarily, McGoran would have retched at the sight of so much blood and guts and singed bodies, but he took the food and consumed it. *I can't believe I have an appetite under these conditions*, he thought. *It's all so incomprehensible.*

McGoran volunteered to join a work party of ten seamen to acquire more antiaircraft ammunition from other ships because the *California* was running out of ammo. The bomb blast had made it impossible to reach one of the main magazines, causing the shortage.

As the men started across the quarterdeck to board a motor launch, several strafing Japanese planes lined up and aimed for the *California*. The planes came in low, firing their machine guns and then circled around for another deadly strafing run. The sailors sprinted out onto the quarterdeck and dragged to shelter those who had been struck by the bullets. Then, as soon as they felt it was safe, McGoran and the rest of the work party dashed for the waiting boat on the other side of the ship.

The launch motored past the capsized *Oklahoma* to the USS *Maryland*. McGoran shouted up to sailors on the battleship's forecastle, begging for extra ammunition, but the work party was ignored. "I guess to them, their problems are far greater than ours," McGoran told his fellow sailors. "Maybe if we had spoken to an officer, we might have been more successful."

The work party gave up and headed to the USS *West Virginia*, which was sinking and on fire. Warrant Officer H. A. Applegate selected five men to go aboard with him. McGoran and the others remained in the launch. As he watched the men walk under the barrels of the big guns, a bomb exploded right next to them. The forecastle erupted in smoke and flames. An officer clad in a white uniform emerged from the smoke, flailing away because he was engulfed in fire. A sailor onboard shouted down to McGoran and the others in the launch, "Get out of here! The ship might blow up at any minute!"

The coxswain backed the launch away from the burning battleship, unaware that he was reversing straight toward one of the exposed giant propellers of the capsized *Oklahoma*.

McGoran yelled at the coxswain, "Reverse your engines!" McGoran and another sailor scrambled to the stern, stuck their legs over the side, and shoved their feet against the battleship's propeller. Groaning from the strain in their leg muscles, they kept the launch from getting damaged.

When their boat finally went forward, they saw that the perimeter of flaming oil on the surface of the water was closing in on them. Just then, they spotted a sailor struggling in the water near amidships of the *West Virginia*. "We're going in after him," the coxswain said. Even though they had been warned that the battleship could explode, he maneuvered the launch between the vessel and the oily fire, allowing the men onboard to rescue the seaman.

The launch then took everyone to the dock at the navy shipyard to look for more ammo. McGoran stopped briefly and stared at the unbelievable scene spanning the harbor. Battleship Row was a mass of destruction, smoke, fire, and mangled steel.

The *California* was sinking and there was nothing anyone could do about it.

McGoran shook his head. *For those who aren't here, no words will adequately describe this,* he thought. *For those of us who are here, no words are necessary.* Snapping out of his reflective moment, he turned to his comrades and said, "Let's get cracking. We have a war to win—and, by God, we're going to win it."

Of those fighting aboard the California, *105 lost their lives and 62 were wounded. Although she sank in shallow waters, leaving only her superstructure above the surface, she was eventually refloated, repaired, and returned to combat. She engaged in significant battles in the South Pacific, including Saipan, Guam, and Okinawa. She sank a Japanese battleship during the victorious Battle of Leyte Gulf off the coast of the Philippines in history's last fight between opposing battleships.*

Fifteen Medals of Honor were awarded for heroic actions during the Pearl Harbor attacks. The California *had four such heroes—more than any other ship in the harbor.*

Jackson Pharris survived the Pearl Harbor attack and was hospitalized for three months before returning to duty. He was awarded the Medal of Honor in 1948 by President Harry Truman "for conspicuous gallantry and intrepidity at the risk of his life above and beyond the call of duty." A destroyer escort was named in his honor. Pharris retired from the military in 1948, got married, and had four children. He died in 1966 at the age of 54 and is buried in Arlington National Cemetery.

Herbert Jones, Thomas Reeves, and Robert Scott were each posthumously awarded the Medal of Honor and had destroyer escorts named after them. Jesse Jewell and William Fleming were each presented with the Navy Cross for their actions.

Howard Haynes, who had been in the brig, carried out his orders so well that he earned a recommendation for retention in the service.

GLOSSARY

A-A short for antiaircraft

ACCOMMODATION LADDER a ladder suspended over the side of a ship, used for boarding from a boat

AFT in, near, or toward the stern of the ship

AFTER that which is farthest aft

AGROUND resting on or touching the bottom of shallow water

ALL HANDS the ship's entire crew, including officers and enlisted personnel

AMIDSHIPS the middle of a ship between the bow and stern

ARMY AIR CORPS forerunner of the United States Air Force

ASAP abbreviation for "as soon as possible"

BARNACLES small shellfish that attach themselves to bottoms of vessels

BATTERY the ship's big guns with turrets

BELOWDECKS any space beneath the ship's main deck

BERTH the space assigned to a ship for anchoring or mooring; also sleeping space for a crewman

BILGE the lowest inner part of a ship's hull

BOATSWAIN (pronounced BO-sun) the person in charge of boats, rigging, and ground tackle aboard ship

BOW the most forward part of a ship

BRASS navy slang for the high-ranking officers

BRIDGE an enclosed structure above the main deck where the ship is operated, steered, and navigated

BRIDGE WING an open-air section of the bridge, used for signaling

BRIG a ship's jail

BULKHEAD a wall in a ship

BULWARK an extension of a ship's sides above the level of the deck

CABIN the living compartment of a ship's commanding officer

CASEMATE an armored compartment in a ship, in which guns are mounted

CENTRAL STATION a warship's communications center

CHIPPER a person who chips old paint and rust off ships

COLORS the national flag (also called ensign); the ceremony of raising and lowering the flag

COMPARTMENT a room in a ship

CONN to direct a ship

CONNING TOWER a warship's armored pilothouse on a raised platform where an officer can conn the vessel and give directions to the helmsman

CORPSMAN an enlisted person in the navy or the Marines trained in giving first aid and basic medical treatment to crewmen

COUNTERFLOOD to deliberately flood compartments on the opposite side of a ship where compartments are already flooded, to keep the ship level

COXSWAIN (pronounced COCK-sun) an enlisted person who steers one of the ship's smaller boats

DECK a ship's floor or platform

DETAIL a group of sailors assigned to a temporary, specific assignment; also known as **PARTY**

DOG a lever or bolt with thumbscrews used for securing a watertight door

DOGGED when the dogs on a watertight door are set

DRY DOCK a narrow basin or vessel that can be filled with water or drained and used for the maintenance and repair of a ship

ECHELON a formation of aircraft in parallel rows, with the end of one row projecting farther in front than the next

ENSIGN the lowest grade of a commissioned officer in the navy; also the ship's national flag

FANTAIL the rounded or fan-shaped part of the main deck at the stern

FORE forward

FORECASTLE (pronounced FOK-sul) the raised deck at the bow of the ship

GALLEY a ship's kitchen

GANGWAY an opening in the bulwark of a ship through which passengers may board

GENERAL QUARTERS an announcement for the crew to prepare for battle

GIG a captain's personal boat

GUN DIRECTOR an enclosure high above the deck that contains equipment and devices that help gunnery crews find their targets

HALYARD a light line used to hoist a flag or pennant

HANDLING ROOM a compartment where sailors arrange and place ammunition onto hoists that deliver the ammo to the guns of a warship

HATCH a covered opening to access a deck

HAWSER a thick rope for mooring, towing, or securing a ship

HELM the wheel used to steer the ship

INCENDIARY BULLET a type of ammunition that contains a compound that starts fires

KEEL the beam that runs the length of, in the center and bottom of, the hull

LADDER narrow, often vertical stairs aboard a ship

LAUNCH a motorboat that operates from a ship

LIBERTY permission granted to a crew member to go ashore for a short time

LIFELINE the top line erected around the edge of any exposed deck to keep sailors from falling overboard

LINE navy term for any rope

LIST when a ship leans to port or starboard

LUCKY BAG certain lockers where lost and found items are kept

MAIN DECK the uppermost continuous deck that extends from bow to stern

MAINMAST the towerlike structure on a warship

MAGAZINE compartment used for storing ammunition

MESS meal or place aboard ship where meals are eaten

MOOR to tie a ship to a pier, quay, buoy, or another vessel

OILSKINS sailors' foul-weather clothing made of heavy cotton waterproofed with oil

OLD SALT navy slang for an older, experienced sailor

ORDNANCE supply and storage of weapons and ammunition

OVERHEAD the underside of a deck that forms the ceiling of a ship's compartment below

PARTY a group of sailors assigned to a temporary, specific assignment; also known as **DETAIL**

PASSAGEWAY a hallway on a ship

PORT the left side of a ship when facing forward

QUARTERDECK part of the main deck near the stern reserved for honors and ceremonies

QUAY (pronounced KEY) a solid structure that juts out into the water like a wharf or pier that is used for loading and unloading ships

READY BOX a container placed near a ship's gun to hold ammunition that can be used immediately

REVETMENT a barricade of earth or sandbags that provides protection for parked planes or prevents them from overrunning when landing

ROUND a single unit of ammunition

SALVO a number of bombs or torpedoes dropped from planes at roughly the same time

SHIPFITTER a person who repairs ships

SICK BAY a ship's hospital or dispensary

SKIVVIES navy slang for men's underwear

STARBOARD the right side of the ship when facing forward

STATION a crewman's or officer's place of duty

STERN the back, or aft, part of a ship

STRAFING machine gun fire from low-flying aircraft

SUPERSTRUCTURE the tall sections of a ship other than masts that rise above the main deck

SWABBY navy slang for a new sailor or one who has a low rank

TURRET an armored, rotating installation that contains mounted guns and gunnery crew on a warship

VOID one of many empty spaces between the inside of a ship's hull and its bulkheads

VOLLEY guns or artillery fired at the same time

WARDROOM the officers' mess room aboard a warship

WATCH a particular duty onboard a ship performed usually over a four-hour period

ZERO a Japanese long-range, single-engine fighter plane

ABOUT THE AUTHOR

Allan Zullo is the author of more than 100 nonfiction books on subjects ranging from sports and the supernatural to history and animals.

He has introduced Scholastic readers to the 10 True Tales series, gripping stories of extraordinary persons who have met the challenges of dangerous, sometimes life-threatening situations. Among the books in the series are *Vietnam War Heroes; World War I Heroes; World War II Heroes; War Heroes: Voices from Iraq; Battle Heroes: Voices from Afghanistan; Young Civil Rights Heroes; FBI Heroes;* and *Heroes of 9/11.* In addition, he has authored five books about the real-life experiences of young people during the Holocaust—*Survivors: True Stories of Children in the Holocaust; Heroes of the Holocaust: True Stories of Rescues by Teens; Escape: Children of the Holocaust; We Fought Back: Teen Resisters of the Holocaust;* and *Young Survivors of the Holocaust.*

Allan, the father of two grown daughters and the grandfather of five, lives with his wife, Kathryn, near Asheville, North Carolina. To learn more about the author, visit his website at www.allanzullo.com.